David J. Trusty
Philippians 3:13-14

Gospel Tidbits

By

David Trusty

Bible verses are from the King James version of the Bible.

This book was printed in the United States of America.

To order additional copies of this book, contact:

David Trusty
104 Hulbert - Box 359
Alger, Ohio 45812-0359
trusty560@roadrunner.com

Published by
FWB Publications

Table of Contents

David Trusty

Foreword

Some of my earliest memories of my father are of him preaching and telling stories, often at the same time. I remember sitting around the kitchen table when friends would come over. My mom would make pot after pot of coffee while my dad told stories one after another. It was more entertaining than anything on television.

My brothers and I have heard some of his stories so many times we know them by heart. Occasionally one of us hears a new one. When this does happen, the story is the first topic of conversation the next time we talk. I remember just last year when my dad and I were driving across Ohio. Outside of Mansfield we passed the old state penitentiary. I asked dad if he knew that parts of Shawshank were filmed there. This prompted a new story. He said he was in that prison when he was a child. One of his relatives was serving time and my grandma took dad for a lunch visit. He said it was scary and left quite an impression on him. I will let him tell the rest of the story.

Some of dad's stories provide practical knowledge and some of them tell of family or historical events. Many of them are funny. Some may sound like "fish" stories or urban legends, but I assure you all of them are true. For years, I have been trying to get him to write them down and with this book, that has happened. Now Grand dad Trusty's stories can be enjoyed by future generations of our family, friends, members, and many others.

Gospel Tidbits Applied to Life

SHALL I WRITE A BOOK?

Our eldest said to me some months ago, "Dad, you ought to write a book." To this I have given thought and will begin the endeavor with the title.

GOSPEL TIDBITS -- No, that may not make it. When almost finished I will ask for help from the four most intelligent people I know. Those four are my wife and our three sons. This makes them very smart because they are related to me.

As you can tell by the above statement I enjoy a good laugh and having fun. And yes, all four of them are intelligent and I love them dearly but, most of all I thank God that He afforded me the privilege to have them in my life.

The four Gospels of Matthew, Mark, Luke, and John were written as the title to each book states before each name "according to". Matthew presented Jesus as a Jew, Mark presented Him as a Servant, Luke presented Him as a man (Son of Man), while John presented Him as God. Each of the four were written at different times with John writing his account many years after the occurrences recorded in it. Looking back he would have a better understanding because now the bigger picture was opened and he could better understand the teachings of Jesus.

I'm Still Trying To Grow Up

Most have probably read or heard the words "Growing old is mandatory while growing up is optional".

In some ways there are times I still feel like a kid at heart. I still enjoy some of the things I did as a child. Many of the physical things I did are no longer within my abilities yet mentally I often think as a teen ager if there is the possibility of getting a laugh from a situation. I never want to stop using that ability because I firmly believe the saying "If you don't use it you lose it". Proverbs 17:22, reads " A merry heart doeth good like a medicine: but a broken spirit drieth the bones". Laughter is a great medicine. It takes the mind away from physical ails and gives relief even if only temporary. I remember hearing folks of my parents generation say "looks like a mule eating saw briars". They were referring to those who looked so sad. I recall a man that I only saw smile one or two times. Two friends who knew him commented about the man. One called him "Stoneface" while the other said if he ever smiled they would need a dust pan to sweep his face up.

Some folks think Christians should always be solemn, serious, and never laugh. There's the story of a young boy sitting in Sunday School class and the teacher was telling them how God was involved in making everything and asked each person to describe something they saw on the way to the church that morning. When his turn came the boy told the class he had seen a Christian mule. His teacher asked why it was a Christian mule and the boy replied, "Because he looked so sad like the other Christians do". That is a sad description of Christianity.

We should present to the world an inspiring, smiling, happy persona for all to see. Because of what Christ did for us and our acceptance of it we have more reason to be viewed in the eyes of the world as the happiest people on earth. I'm happy because I'm on my way to Heaven, a place the Son of God Himself went to prepare for me and one day He will return to earth to take me there with Him. The Inspirations Quartet from Bryson City sang these word, "I'm so happy as I travel on the bright road to glory land, and I'm living so my light for Jesus will shine.....". We should exude happiness and do all we can to spread it to all. The late actor Don Knotts played in the western "The Shakiest Gun In The West" as a dentist who said "I'm gonna spread dental health through the west like a plague". Every Christian should be trying to spread true happiness like a plague.

Since I have been in the ministry for 45, years I feel I have great memories from which to recall as well as from some sad situations. I have been blessed to hear some great preachers and to read sermons of many men who were close to God in their daily work and walk and this ultimately added to their ability to be a success in reaching and relating the gospel to others. Therefore I shall discuss them first.

Preachers

Apostle Paul gives us the preacher's qualifications. In the New Testament, the terms "bishop," "pastor," and "elder" all mean the same thing. Bishop means "overseer," and the elders had the responsibility of overseeing the work of the church. "Elder" is the translation of the Greek word *presbutes*, which means "an old man." Paul used the word presbytery in 1 Tim 4:14, referring to the "eldership" of the assembly that ordained Timothy. Elders and bishops are two names for the same office and were required to be mature people with spiritual wisdom and experience. "Pastor" means "shepherd," one who guides and cares for God's flock. Paul gave sixteen qualifications for a **man** to meet in order to hold this office. Notice the emphasis I place on the word "man". I do so because God's book teaches, especially in Paul's writings, that the woman has not that right or authority.

Types of preachers

The "Wild Man"

I read in a clean joke book of a man who went to Seminary and was required while there to take a course in "Diction". The first day of class everyone was given twenty marbles and a list of words to pronounce clearly. A simple task for most of the words. The catch was they must put the twenty marbles in their mouth before beginning the task of pronunciation. The next day they were given more difficult words to speak but were allowed to remove one marble from their mouth at the start of class. This procedure continued each day until on the last day of class they removed the final marble. The point being when they had lost all their marbles they were then qualified to preach. Some preachers I have listened to I think took that course because it was evident they had "lost all their marbles". The book of Proverbs has as its main purpose the instruction that we are never to stop learning. It is to be a lifetime task and should be enjoyable as we accomplish it. The closer our personal relationship with the Lord the more blessed we feel each time we discover something from the Bible we have overlooked in the past. When I learn something previously missed in studies I can hardly wait to work in into the message next time I preach.

I knew a preacher who actually hit people while speaking. On different occasions he slapped one man's face, knocked the breath out of another man, hit a dear friend who was blind, Brother Hubert Davis, on the thigh just above the knee so hard that Hubert's wife said when they got ready for bed that night he had a hand imprint in red on his leg.

Years ago I spoke in a church on average once a month. Their pastor often said "It's time to turn the preacher loose." Immediately my mind formed a picture of a wild man in a cage whom they were going to set free for a little while. The preacher should always speak legibly and distinct enough he can be easily understood even in times when he is lifted emotionally in a part of his message. He should always have himself under control emotionally and certainly be well prepared before stepping into the pulpit.

"The Open Letter Preacher"

This is the individual who "just opens up and lets'er fly". Some compare their style to ranting and raving. They speak with a high volume both audibly and of words.

In 1967, I heard Brother Ellis Layne say something that helped me so much through the years of ministry. Brother Ellis said sometimes a preacher will preach a really good sermon and turn around and pour water on it. He never had to explain to me what he meant. Quite simply if the preacher doesn't know when to quit he can undo everything the sermon accomplished. I learned in a public speaking course I took in college something along the same line Brother Ellis Layne spoke of. When you get up to speak obey these guidelines:

> Tell the listeners what you are going to say.

> Say it.

> Tell them what you said.

Then shut up. After you have made the points of the message don't ramble on and on or it will kill the message.

"The Shot Gun Preacher"

These may read a scripture and sometimes never mention that subject again or may not even tell you the subject. They seem to never hook anything in the message together and go on and on. Some of this I attribute to lack of preparation and study, not knowing the subject well enough to instruct others.

Some of the best teachers I have known were in the military and some of them at the time, the early 1960s, had no more than a high school diploma and some without a diploma. However, they knew their subject well and their goal and rewards of their efforts were the same, to see their students grasp the subject they taught. Each preacher should have the dedication these men had. Emphasis placed at the right place and time is necessary as is thorough explanation of difficult passages of scripture.

"The Airplane Preacher"

This was a title Brother Hubert Davis used. We never discussed exactly what he meant by the title because our acquaintance was close enough that I knew what he meant. Those who felt they were smarter and came across to the listeners as being somewhat arrogant. The audience perceives this when it is present. I belong to the Free Will Baptist denomination and early in the ministry I met some of these. Even in our denomination I have found two groups that qualify for airplane status. Some of our Bible College graduates come across this way. Only a few; but some. The second group is comprised of those pastors who served their churches without a salary or as bi-vocational pastors and their church grew to be able to place them on a full salary. Some folks can sense an array of arrogance about these men. I think it wonderful for every church to be able to provide all the needs of the pastor and his family. Certainly God's word teaches it should be so. However I also have an abundance of respect for the many who have never drawn a salary and yet have been faithful to their congregation namely because of what they had in their heart by counting it one of the highest honors of God's work to be asked to pastor and doing the job with the utmost of humility.

Brother Hurtis Stone of Mansfield, Ohio mentioned once at Ohio's State Convention to clarify full time and part time pastors. I agree with him on the definitions. Being on salary by your church doesn't make you any more of a full time pastor than the man who works at a secular job and still manages to do everything needed to be done by the pastor. I feel he is more than full time.

Some people pay more attention to what the preacher does while speaking than they do to what he says. They feel his actions are what makes a good message. Some speakers run, some jump, climb on pew backs, take off their shoes and do other things. That should not be what impresses the hearer. It should be what he says. One lady met a pastor of another church one Monday in the local supermarket and was bragging to him about the sermon her pastor gave the previous day. "It was the best I ever heard." This pastor asked what the message was about. She said, "I don't remember but it was great". Something is wrong in this situation. I hope for her pastor's sake it was her memory.

The Barking Preacher

My Grandma Conley used a term I saw demonstrated all during my youth. The preacher who barks. I knew an elder gentleman who told of attending the same church my Mother's parents attended. He told me when the preacher started his sermon that he kept hearing a dog bark. The old fellow said he looked everywhere even getting down on his knees to look under the pews. He said when getting off his knees after looking under pews as he was sitting back down he realized there wasn't a dog in the church. He finally figured out it wasn't an animal at all. It was the preacher.

I decided long ago that the reason some people do this is because they have heard someone else do it and that is how it is supposed to be. Granny Conley called it the "Baptist Bark". I don't think she had been around those who did this before she and Grandpa got together. Both had lost previous mates. Granny's first husband was a school teacher and a person of culture.

I ask a simple question based on what the Lord told Ananias the disciple from Damascus when instructed to go meet with Saul of Tarsus (later called Apostle Paul). Acts 9:15, reads "Go thy way: for he is a chosen vessel unto me, to bear my name before the Gentiles, and kings, and the children of Israel:" The Lord is telling Ananias that

He has chosen Saul to go before the most educated and highest political people in the world at the time. I ask if Paul barked like a dog what would have been their reaction? I think that what Festus told Paul in Acts 26:24, "Thou art beside thyself; much learning doth make thee mad." would have certainly made Festus feel completely justified in his statement even after Paul had turned in that conversation to King Agrippa. Probably the Apostle would have been laughed to scorn.

Some preachers have a habit of using what I call "fill in" words while they are thinking of their next statement. This can become such a bad habit it will cause a complete mess up at times. We have what I personally call "Glory to God, Hallelujah, Amen" speakers. One fellow stood to give a testimony in church and it went like this. "Me and my wife were driving down the road the other day, *hallelujah.* We had a car wreck, *glory to God.* Through my wife through the windshield, *amen.* Cut her tongue of, *praise the Lord.*" Usually they place special emphasis on the last portion of whatever they tell. If this was true and had I have been present to hear it spoken like this I'm sure I would have rolled out of the seat to the floor laughing so hard. I get tickled easily and the last place I wish to get that way is in a church service.

If we speak legibly with intelligence and have some dignity about us we represent the Lord better as His ambassadors.

Reverend

I don't like to be called Reverend. Some preachers relish in the title, some take it personal and are offended if they are not recognized or referred to by the title.

This word appears only once in all the Bible in Psalm 111:9, the term reverence denotes respect; which must be held for God in all we do.

My preference to not be called Reverend is because of its

use in Scripture is referring to the Almighty. He is the one, the only one worthy of the title as far as I am concerned. Certainly all preachers should live so as to be respected by those who know them. Instead of wanting to be revered we need to desire to be recognized for our humility, a subject I address later.

Who Am I Going To Marry?

After the gift of God's Son, I think family has to rank second. Family started as a gift of the Lord. When God saw that it was not good for Adam to be alone. He made "an help meet" for him. So often it is said a help mate. Genesis 2:18, plainly says God said He would make "an help meet" for him. The word help needs no defining as it is obvious God was making for man someone to be a help to and for him. The word meet means suitable for. So God made for Adam someone who was suitable for him. Someone suitable to help Adam.

As a teenager when I received Christ into my life I knew that someday I would want to marry and have a family. Since I never claimed to be the sharpest knife in the drawer I knew I needed God's help in choosing the person to be my wife. Though I had already met her I had no idea Mary would be the one. I met Mary between my Sophomore and Junior years in high school. Her oldest sister, Louise, lived across the street and a couple houses north of us. Her sister invited my older sister, Karen to go to Kentucky with them to visit and she had met Mary there. Later Mary, two of her sisters, and two brothers came to spend a couple weeks with Louise and her family. When they arrived Karen went over to see them and in a little while she and Mary came back to our house. I was going out the front door as they were coming in. I didn't pay much attention as I was in a hurry. I did notice she was quite pretty. Mary came back the next summer for a visit and I still wasn't that interested even though I noticed again how pretty she was. However when she returned in June 1962, after I had graduated I really took notice of how attractive she was. She had the most beautiful brown eyes I have ever seen. Today, after forty-eight years of being married to her they remain as they were the first time I ever noticed them. She also had beautiful dark brown hair which over the years I probably had a great deal to do with turning it silver. Sometimes now I wake in the middle of the night and just look at her sleeping and think of her creation level. The Bible teaches that God made man a little lower than the angels. Mary was and still is just a minute notch below angel status. But closer than I would ever consider myself to be. When I was a teen one family show on television was "My Three Sons". It was enjoyable and aired for a lot of years then went into syndication and still we can occasionally see episodes of it. Mary and I have lived personally that particular title.

There is the story of a man saying he had been married for twenty-six years and didn't regret one day of it. The day he didn't regret was June 23, 1968. If he only had one day without regret his marriage must have been extremely miserable. The phrase "they lived happily ever after" only applies in fairy tales. Every marriage has a few ups and downs. The forty-eight years Mary and I have been married doesn't seem that long. I guess that time really does fly when you are having fun. I learned that no two persons see everything exactly alike. As a result disagreements arise and some couples do not have the dedication or commitment to their marriage vows to allow it to pass. Forgiveness is an essential element in each marriage along with a desire to make the union succeed.

The morning after our wedding I looked at her and thought "What in the world have I done? The rest of my life......". I wasn't already disappointed. It was then I first realized the commitment we had made. I still have that same commitment today and intend always keeping it. Mary has been, is, and always will be everything I could ever want. Regularly I thank God for her.

Recently we were in a Wal Mart. When we entered she went one direction to check on something she was interested in while I went another direction for the one item I was after. When I finished checking for my item I stepped to the end of the short isle it was in and began scanning all directions for Mary. Two employees, a man and a woman approached where I stood and one said "There's somebody looking for something". I said, "I'm looking for my wife", and she asked what she looked like. I said "When I married her forty eight years ago she had ...". The lady interrupted saying "You don't know what she looks like, do you?" I told her about the most beautiful brown eyes and dark brown hair that I had turned gray. She then pointed to my chin seeing my beard is gray she says, "Looks like she did a little something to you, too."

Gospel Singers Mentality

Just from the above phrase many have no idea what I'm referring to. I have been blessed to hear some of the finest most beautiful gospel singing anyone could want to hear. My favorite of all full time gospel groups has been for forty years the Inspirations Quartet from Bryson City, North Carolina, especially before Archie Watkins retired from the group. Local groups I hold in higher esteem than the professional groups for simple reasons they do it without expecting to make a living from it, They sing strictly for God's glory. They know they are limited in the area and distances they can avail themselves to churches. Most ask no guarantee for financial compensation.

The gospel singers mentality is many of those who sing seem to think that everyone present who sings should sing in every service. Free Will Baptists have District Associations and/or Conferences. These are churches who voluntarily unite to form a Conference to help and assist the sister churches in whatever need may arise. These Conferences have authority for the licensing and ordaining of ministers, the best part is the churches fellowship with each other. Most Conferences have scheduled times of the year they meet with the number of meetings varying from one Conference to the other.

Sometimes the singing groups from several of the churches in the Conference will be in attendance and some from one group thinks everyone or every group should get to sing. It seems to me they are thinking that singing should be the primary emphasis of the entire meeting.

A friend pastoring in Indiana nearly forty years ago told of seeing someone they knew who attended another church that told him their church had such a good service that the pastor didn't have time to preach. My friend told them "Then you got cheated". He certainly told the truth.

Please don't misunderstand me. I love good singing and know the need for it but know the primary way to touch the hearts of people is by the Word of God. Paul wrote to the church at Corinth telling them how worship service should be, saying everyone hath a psalm, etc. We need always to use common sense in order not to in this day tire people out and make sure the proper need is met in each service. This is what the Lord wants.

1 Cor 14:26, tells us the form of worship "How is it then, brethren? when ye come together, every one of you hath a psalm, hath a doctrine, hath a tongue, hath a revelation, hath an interpretation. Let all things be done unto edifying".

Paul speaks of how each may wish to sing or tell something personal but the emphasis of the verse is in the last sentence. Let everything done in the worship service be done to the edifying of the church as a whole not the individual.

Everything in the worship service should be geared to lead to the sermon due to the importance of the Word of God. His Word is how we are fed and grow spiritually as well as touch the hearts of those not saved and draw them to Christ.

Looking For A Church

For different reasons people make decisions about what church they are going to attend. Ohio Free Will Baptist Executive Secretary Edwin Hayes once said "People shop for a church like going to the mall". That is for sure.

What to look for in a church

A newly converted Christian needs a home church to attend where they can be fed from the Word of God. Since some newly come to the faith were not reared in a church atmosphere and are not aware of their spiritual needs here are some guidelines.

First priority should be finding a church where there is intelligent preaching that is upholding God's Word keeping the standard recorded in the Bible while lifting the banner of Christ high.

People should always look for a friendly church. You need to feel the welcoming spirit of the members. Years ago a church was having a revival and two men visited because one of the members had invited them. The only person to acknowledge the two visitors was the man who invited them. One of the visitors said to the other after the service that if not for the person inviting them and being glad they attended no one else knew they were there. Needless to say neither of the two visitors came back.

To the new convert the initial greeting from many of the members might be the thing that impresses them most about a church. Many years ago someone told me that a barber can be the worst in the area but still have a thriving business if he has an outgoing personality, is friendly, treats everyone with respect, and makes them feel he cares about them. This definitely works for a church. Most people enjoy good singing. Having great singing talent is a tremendous blessing to a church. However the primary focus of every church should be the Word of God. Selecting a church with this available can be more difficult for the new convert than for someone who has been saved several years and studied the Bible. The reason being most young converts are not familiar with the Bible enough and this can cause them to make the wrong choice because of that. When someone new comes to a church all the members should go out of their way to welcome them.

Fellowship and worship are important in each local church. Amos 3:3, asks "Can two walk together, except they be agreed?" To have fellowship with someone, means to gain or share information, experience, wisdom, serenity, and freedom through life's journey. Example: My heavenly father and I fellowship together in that I learn from Him as He shares with me.

Worship is to be the focus of the church meeting. Some southern folks I know don't say "going to church", but "going to meetin' ". Attending a time of fellowship during which God is praised should be what church is all about. One lady asks her husband on the way home from church "Did you see the dress Mrs. Jones had on today?" His answer was "no". She then asks about another lady's hat to which she got another answer of "No". She then scolds her husband by saying "A lot of good it does you to go to church." We attend church to worship the Lord, not to see or be seen.

To Be Baptized Or Not To Be Baptized?

In late 1967, I was invited to preach at a country church south of Wabash, Indiana. After the sermon at the invitation a lady came forward, accepted Christ, and said she wished to be baptized, **Right Now**. She asked Rev. Richard Pelphery and myself to perform it. She was a rather large person and obviously there was the need for two men to accomplish this. I weighed about two hundred thirty-five pounds which was in excess of Richard by one hundred and ten pounds. The leaves were all gone from the trees and there had been a solid frost that particular Sunday morning with the temperature remaining below freezing. I had not come prepared for a baptism service and brought no extra clothing. Pastor Melvin Staggs had a son my size and asked for me to swing by his home to change into some old clothes. After changing we went to the farm pond where Richard and I would carry out this woman's desire for immediate baptism. My vehicle was a 1960, Thunderbird that sat quite low and the ruts in the lane to the pond caused my tail pipes to drag and come off. I knew I could fix that problem with not much effort. I never knew I would be facing another problem.

Richard waded into the water which had ice frozen just shy of one fourth of an inch thick. Freshly frozen ice that thin can be sharp and Richard received several small cuts as he pushed the ice out of the way. Now I hold this lady's arm and lead her into the water.

Let me here explain the baptism process and how it is carried out. Baptism as taught by Scripture represents something in particular. It represents a death, a burial, and a resurrection. Death is represented as the person being baptized has died out to their old way of life and sinfulness. Burial is the immersion of the new believer in water being buried with Christ. The resurrection is after the immersion you are raised from this burial to walk in a "newness of life". We no longer do the sinful things we did in the past and endeavor to walk in Jesus steps. It is best for the person or persons administering baptism to be standing in water about waist deep. This makes the physical effort of the baptism easier.

Back to the Indiana farm pond: As I lead this woman out to where Richard is she stops where the water is about knee deep. She begins what sounds like mumbling (I assumed she was praying) then after a few minutes she says "let's go on out". I escort her to where Richard is standing, turn her around so those on the bank of the pond can see her face, then she starts mumbling again. This lasted for about five minutes during which time I look over at skinny little Richard and his lower jaw is bouncing up and down from being cold. Now I enjoy a good laugh and sometimes it doesn't take a lot to get me started laughing so I look away from Richard. I sneak another glance at Richard and only a glance because I'm about to lose it thinking "what dance is Richard's jaw doing?" I knew it wasn't the twist or the limbo and decide it's doing the jerk. Before I can erupt in laughter the lady brought me back to reality by saying "The Lord don't want me to be baptized today" and walks out of the pond. This startled Richard so much his jaw stopped doing the jerk. He and I looked at one another and shrugged then walked out of the water too.

Never have I experienced anything even remotely similar to that day. I yet had to jack up my car and slip the tail pipes back on while lying on the cold ground with the clothing on the lower half of my body getting hard from freezing. Then we returned to Melvin's where I changed clothes to change back. I told one of the brethren that day that if I was ever in the area again and this woman wanted me to help baptize her that she would definitely be going under the water even if I had to bulldog her to get the job done.

I still laugh every time I recall this and still can see Richard's jaw bouncing.

In the early 1950s, I remember the church Dad started

baptized a large number of new converts in the winter time. There was several inches of ice they chopped through at the creek on Sugar Street. Someone called the Lima News and they were there taking pictures which appeared in the next edition. I always thought the reporter had most likely never witnessed anything like this and came out of curiosity. Many people stopped to watch and some said that everyone would probably get pneumonia from being wet in the freezing weather. Whether folks came to view from being curious or whatever one thing was accomplished by the article in the paper. Other people began coming there to church. Thank God.

Things Learned As A Child

Bugs Bunny is not real.

Spinach didn't do for me what it does for Popeye the Sailor Man.

You're not going to be every ones favorite.

Life simply isn't fair. We can't wait for our big break to come. We must make it.

To be successful requires hard work which some people are not willing to do.

The same God who made you and me made all people, black, white, yellow, brown, red, and if there be any others He made them too. So if we are made by the same God and he loves us all equally there is no room for prejudice by any race and this pleases God.

Many people pick favorites. These can be a favorite shirt, dress, pair of pants, as well as favorite person.

Doing your best sometimes isn't good enough to make the team. I remember hearing former Pittsburg Steelers quarterback Terry Bradshaw giving an answer to a simple question that can apply to everything we do or face in life. He was asked about the ability to throw a spiral pass with the football. He said, "It's a God given talent; but, you can improve on it." So we should always try to improve our abilities.

 Be honest in all your dealings. It is the only way to be.

No one admires a liar because you can't trust them. Though we think a little "white lie" isn't all that bad. The Bible teaches if we are guilty of the least we are guilty of the whole. King David after lusting for Bathsheba called for her, committed adultery with her, trying to prevent being found out went deeper into sin by getting her husband Uriah drunk and ultimately had him killed in battle. So, what we may consider a small sin soon begins to grow and in the end ensnares us and takes us to deeper levels of the devil's kingdom.

Childhood was a great time with plenty to occupy our attention. Pets, sports, television, playing with friends, fishing and hunting, and sometimes just doing nothing.

Television had good cartoons then with Heckle and Jeckle, Mighty Mouse always getting the best of Oil Can Harry, and the different Looney Tunes. American Bandstand was on weekdays shortly after school and on weekends there was Gunsmoke and Bonanza, both great westerns. Friends in Lima told of a man who would strap on his holster and pistol Saturday nights to draw against Marshall Dillon. Once he forgot to unload his weapon and shot his TV. Whether he won or not I don't know but it had to be an expensive lesson for him.

Camping with other boys I enjoyed probably more than any activity. Usually we stayed awake all night keeping the fire going and cooking whatever food brought. The summer between my sophomore and junior years of high school a large group of guys were camping and one of them was eighteen years of age. That made him old enough to buy 3.2, beer. We chipped in our money and he went to town and got some for us. My intent was to get drunk, a sensation I wished to experience. When Bill returned with the brew I opened one and took a big swallow. I nearly puked. After a couple minutes I took another drink. Right then and there my drinking career was over as I gave the remainder of mine to my cousin. The only thing I ever tasted worse than beer is liquid potassium. How people think beer tastes good I can't understand. A few months after that experience I accepted Christ into my life and as a result have never wanted anything to do with alcoholic drinks.

As teens in the late 1950s, we boys were interested in cars, especially fast ones. Many boys and some grown men who had cars of their own had names painted on the rear quarter panels. A few names were Tragedy, Running Wild, and Aspirin Taster. A red 1957 T-Bird, not a local car "The Red Bird" also had a Continental Kit and was something to see.

Success

Most who want to *be* end up never being. The late comedian Dave Gardner told one of two fellows digging in a ditch. One just shoveled all day because he liked to shovel. The other leaned on his shovel and kept saying "One of these days I'm gonna own this construction company". Years later the same fellow was still leaning on a shovel handle saying the same thing and the other who liked to shovel owned the company, had a new home, "wall to wall maids, hot and cold running towels", new cars, and all the things that go with enjoying success. Personally, I define success as being happy in what you do. It isn't measured in dollars and cents as most feel it to be. There have been a few times I was without a dollar to my name and still felt successful. This was because I was happy in the work I did, the family I have, the bills were paid, but most of all Jesus was living in me. That is real success just in knowing God is pleased with your efforts.

Success takes perseverance which some are unwilling to use. A daughter and her boy friend came to her dad to ask permission to marry. The dad said no, that she was too young. Her reply was "Daddy let us try it". Evidently she was unaware that marriage is not to be tried out like an automobile. Marriage is a commitment that takes perseverance for it to be successful. Years ago Mary and I had a visit from friends who had been married several years less than we had at that particular time. He and I were outside in nice weather talking while she and Mary were in the house doing something probably with the boys. He commented to me that they had not had a single argument during their marriage. I never said anything about doubting his word but my mind was thinking it. Sometime later I mentioned to Mary what he said on that visit and how it was hard to imagine it to be true, especially from our own experiences in our marriage. We have had a few arguments and still have disagreements though they are certainly not often. Since we both have a bit of a stubborn streak we will never see everything exactly one hundred percent alike. When I told Mary of the conversation I had with the other fellow she told me that on the same visit his wife was telling her of the different arguments they had. Maybe in his mind he never felt there was ever any disagreement on anything. If you are always right there is no need for someone to not agree with you. The problem is no individual is always right on everything. King Solomon was the most intelligent person ever to or will live and he made some mistakes. Recognizing this we know all of us err sometimes and need to persevere. Perseverance should be made in every aspect of our lives. Work, marriage, raising children, our relationship with God, and relationships with people. These all need perseverance.

As a pastor it is an essential element in watching over the particular flock the Lord has assigned us to.

Continuing to be obedient to His will may sometimes call for us to stay where we are instead of accepting a larger church. I had the opportunity in the late 1970s, to pastor a church in another state which was quite large, had lots of talented members, and a growth potential I recognized to be tremendous. After several conversations and visits preaching for them I had to make a decision. Am I going to uproot my family and move nearly two hundred miles where they would need to make new friends and make the adjustments necessary? I'm ready, willing, and able to uproot and move because of the potential I envisioned in that church. I knew I could work with and for these people and felt it would be a great fit for both that church and myself. However I have to talk it over with my Superior to see if it is okay for me to accept this offer. My Superior wasn't Mary or any other individual. I had to pray and see if this is what God wants. I never thought to tell Mary to start packing while I prayed about it. I knew if the Lord doesn't approve the offer I would have to decline. He said I couldn't go. I was disappointed but willing to accept His answer. It took that church several months to get a pastor and the one God did send was a true blessing to that church. He accomplished more than I feel I could have.

Why wasn't I allowed to go? I never worried about it after receiving assurance not to take their offer. The answer to this question took some passing of time before I saw it. We had always prayed for the Lord to make a way for us to send our boys to college. The Lord worked it out so they could. Mary was hired at Ohio Northern University, a very prestigious private University. For employees there was a tuition remission program through which Alvin, Bo, and Troy all were able to graduate. Our total cost for tuition for all three was twenty percent of one year's tuition for one person.

Not uprooting the family and most of all being obedient to God's will was a success that gained bachelor's degrees for our three sons. Simply said "Success comes in different ways, some of which we don't see until later".

I want my greatest success to recognized at the end of life's journey. I want it to be recognized by He who gives eternal recognition. The Apostle Peter said in1 Peter 5:4, " And when the chief Shepherd shall appear, ye shall receive a crown of glory that fadeth not away."

This will be an eternal reward and recognition for all who have faithfully served the Lord.

If the only success a person has is financial reward, fame for whatever he or she accomplished in their field of endeavor and never sought to please our Creator they will have been completely unsuccessful.

It has been said that everyone has fifteen minutes of fame. Whether this be true or not I never researched to find out. Whatever a person credits with that fame should be the determining factor if what they did is true success.

Making NFL footballs for Wilson Sporting Goods gave me one opportunity that to me described success as best I ever witnessed. Starting with Super Bowl twenty six the

NFL began the NFL Experience inviting Wilson Sporting Goods to demonstrate making the NFL footballs. The first NFL Experience was held at the Minneapolis Convention Center in January 1992 prior to Super Bowl XXVI, and I was there for Wilson. The following year in Pasadena, California, we were given the opportunity to attend the Athletes In Action Super Bowl Breakfast. Tom Landry was the featured speaker, Bart Starr the emcee, singer and movie star Pat Boone was there, as well as many sports figures. The one I enjoyed most was the backup quarterback for the Buffalo Bills, Frank Reich. He had led the Bills in the second half of the AFC championship game to the biggest comeback so far in the NFL when he outscored the Huston Oilers during the second half and overtime by a margin of thirty-five to three to win forty-one to thirty-eight.

During the program that morning Frank made a statement I have never forgotten because of the impression it left in my mind and heart. "I don't want to be remembered as a football player who was a Christian. I want to be remembered as a Christian who happened to play football." What a great definition of success. Having all your priorities in proper order is what his words told me.

Having the opportunity to attend the Athletes In Action event that Super Bowl week gave me the opportunity to tell people that I had been privileged to have breakfast with legendary football coach Tom Landry. However I always followed that statement by telling them the coach probably didn't even know I was there because there were hundreds in attendance.

Another benefit in working for Wilson was I had the opportunity to meet John Elway, my favorite quarterback of all time. I was amazed at his size. Behind the huge linemen he seemed smaller. All the years he played and the hits he took he had to be in tremendous condition. The smile he always had makes me feel he was enjoying what he was doing. I am thankful for him that he won two Super Bowls before retiring from playing.

I also got to hear Joe Gibbs speak at the NFL Experience in Minneapolis. This was a treat even though it was only a few words from a Christian coach whom I admired.

A Family That Makes Dad So Proud

God blessed us to have three sons. Though they are similar in many ways they are yet different in other ways. The eldest, Alvin Dean, we jokingly refer to as the family genius. He always grasped things quickly and has a competitiveness I admire tremendously. Alvin was born eleven minutes before midnight December 31, 1965, at Homestead Air Force Base Hospital approximately thirty miles south of Miami, Florida. He was due on the nineteenth of the month which was my birthday but was twelve days late. Mary has been one of the most proficient persons I know in everything except childbirth. She always ran behind schedule in this area. She is an excellent cook, housekeeper, mother, wife, babysitter, worker and anything else you can mention. She bakes the best homemade biscuits I have ever tasted. They melt in your mouth. But she was always a little slow in the timely birthing department. However, when she did deliver she brought forth the best.

I was in the U. S. Air Force from July 1962, through July 1966. We were both thrilled when the doctor confirmed she was expecting our first. I wrote a short letter to her sister Joyce who was still at home telling her that "Mary was going to have kittens".

The day Alvin was born she awoke from the onset of labor. I rushed her to the base hospital where I was promptly told to go home and wait, they will call after it's over. I went home to be by the phone. Being an impatient person after a couple hours I called to check on her. Reply, "No change". Another couple hours go by and I call again. Reply, "No change". Going stir crazy because of my impatience I went to my part time job off base. With my base pay being $ 137.00, a month I picked up a part time employment opportunity in order to provide better and a few extras for us. Nowadays I tell people I got the part time job so we could eat. At that time living in south Florida was double the cost of living in Ohio. I went to my part time and called the hospital for an update and give them the number to call me there. Reply, "No change". I left at 10:00PM, that night returning home called the hospital to inform them I am at home and to call there. Reply, "No change". So I got ready and went to bed. You can probably tell by now I knew nothing about the process of giving birth because it had not entered my mind that there could be anything wrong. I just went about the everyday things thinking that this sure is taking a long time. I went to sleep and the phone awoke me shortly after midnight and I could hear the sound of fireworks going off outdoors. The nurse asked me if I was going to come see my son. Telling her I would be right there she cautioned me to drive carefully and not speed. I went in the hospital and the nurse was taking him for circumcision and introduced he and I before I had gotten to see Mary. Alvin had curly hair when he was born and I noticed he was kind of red and had the Trusty's nose. I went in to see Mary. She asked if I had seen him yet. My reply, "Yeah, what took you so long?" I looked at Mary and said "You're flat again."

I look back now and I'm ashamed at how immature I was at that time. I never gave consideration to the idea that Mary may have a girl. I knew we were going to have a boy and I fully intended to name him after my dad. I lost Dad when I was ten and cherished his memory and his reputation. From the time shortly after losing Dad I had made up my mind that my first child would be a boy and would be named Alvin. Mary was fully receptive to the idea and added Dean as the middle name. She liked that name and as long as Alvin was first I was okay. During this time we lived in a mobile home in the country about ten miles from the base. I rented it from Frank, whom I was told was the third largest fruit grove owner in the country at the time. He was a nice fellow I had met through Snuffy, the man who owned the service station where I worked part time. Mary spent almost all her waking hours with Alvin. She read to him constantly, showed him things and told him what they were. I look back and see how this helped his IQ. Years later I read an article that told a child's learning potential was actually developed in the first few months of its life. I worked at the base from 0730, to 1600 hours (7:30 AM to 4:00 PM). After Alvin was born the garage where I worked contracted with Dade County to buy gas and oil for their vehicles so we needed to keep it open 24/7. Instead of hiring a new person for the midnight shift I took it myself working from eleven at night until six in the morning. Then I would go home, sometimes sleep twenty minutes, shower, and go to the base. This gave me time to spend about three fourths of an hour with Alvin before getting about five hours sleep and starting off again on the midnight shift. Mary was totally wrapped up in Alvin and we see the benefits of that today in Alvin's career.

Bo is our second son. His name is David Vinson. Mary wanted him named after me and I wanted him to have the name Vinson in it because of one of the dearest deacons I had known, Vinson Williams. Vince had told me things about my Dad I never knew and gave me a little bit of an insight to who and what my Dad really was. Vince was faithful and dedicated to the Lord and his local church. God unexpectedly called him home in early 1967, leaving a void which I had to overcome. I think of Vince from time to time and always picture in my mind the unique smile he always had. When we brought young David Vinson home from Lima Memorial Hospital Alvin was waiting and when Mary showed him to Alvin she said "This is Bubby". Alvin repeated it incorrectly by saying "Bubbo". Everyone thought it was cute and started calling him so and over time it became "Bo".

Probably most parents have special memories of each of their children. This is true of our boys. One of my favorite of Bo was one day when Alvin was in Kindergarten and went only in the afternoon. We had to take them to school and they would ride the bus home at the end of the day. I was home one day and drove him to school. We arrived early and Alvin saw some of his friends and classmates on the playground. Bo rode with us that day and as Alvin ran to be with the other kids Bo was watching and said as sincerely as I've ever heard any preschooler say anything

"Next year I'm gonna have me some friends". I noticed the sadness of the look on his face as though he was missing out on something he was not yet allowed to have. I had to fight back tears. Those words still come to mind regularly when I think of Bo and how he made them come true not just the next year when he got to go to kindergarten but he is still adding to the list of his friends. He has coached several sports beginning with high school football when he was in college. He earned varsity letters in four sports in high school and as a result has a good grasp of more than just the basics in football and basketball. At various times he voluntarily went from coaching high school to the junior high level in these two sports and been quite successful at both levels.

I realized years ago that athletic talent in school goes in cycles. Usually, the only schools that have top notch teams year after year after year are religious schools that recruit talent from other area schools. These schools deny then that they recruit. In Ohio with "Open Enrollment" coming into being some years ago I have no objections to an athlete wishing to attend a neighboring school to play a sport with a winner. The only problem I see is when coaches and alumni try to persuade someone to come play in that district.

One of the local football programs I admire tremendously is that of the Kenton Wildcats. Their coach, Mike Mauk, is an absolute class act, knows how to win, and has instilled through his success an inspiration within boys at a young age to desire to be a part of this football program. Coach Mauk has with him an excellent staff wherein it is obvious they know their jobs well. The season of Kenton's which I admire most is after having two consecutive state titles in Division IV, and losing almost all the talent of that team came back the following season having to move up to Division III, due to enrollment numbers and finished the season as state runners-up. That speaks volumes of Coach Mauk and his coaching staff. With all his success Coach Mauk never forgets those who played for him. He earned their respect in many ways and remains loyal to his players long after they have moved on.

Bo is the same type as Coach Mike Mauk and this makes my shirt size swell when I think of it. Many of those who played for him or he had in the classroom never forget him. Some went into the military and when they come back to the area on leave they come visit him. Last fall Bo forwarded to me an email from a former student who thanked him for the inspiration he had been to him saying if not for Bo he would not be where he is today. He went to college, became a teacher, and presently is an assistant football coach with one of the larger schools in a suburb of Columbus, Ohio that was having a great season. Touching lives is the most important aim in life. It's great to inspire athletes, students, workers, friendships; but nothing is as important as touching lives and inspiring them to look to Jesus Christ. That is my greatest personal desire.

Our youngest is Troy Earnest. As usual Mary was behind schedule delivering him, by eighteen days. Troy was born after church on Sunday night December 20, 1970. Mary said she didn't feel like going to church that night. It never entered my mind she was going into labor. Again I wanted and expected another boy. Mary always wanted a girl and as I look back a part of me wishes she had gotten one. Which of the boys would I trade for a daughter? No way. Each time after giving birth she was well satisfied with having had a boy. Each of the boys had noticeably different personalities. They played well together getting along most of the time. I said most of the time because kids will surely be kids. After they were grown they let us in on a few of their private escapades that we had been unaware of when they were happening. Neither Mary nor I would have been very understanding. But I had done things when I was growing up that were classified along those lines and escaped punishment. I guess all kids get away with a few actions kept secret. When Troy was seven or eight, the boys along with the sons of the Pastor of the Methodist church made an igloo at the home of a friend. Naturally they wanted to sleep in it that night and enjoy the comfort it provided. Troy explained to Mom and Dad how many could get inside the igloo. Though I don't recall the numbers he gave the terms I will never forget. They could get one more in it "scrunched" than they could "unscrunched".

Troy always thought he could do anything his brothers could and always pretty much held his own. When they played football together Alvin always had Troy on the other team it seemed. Troy being the smallest was made to hike the ball. Alvin loved that because at first he was nearly twice the size of Troy and as soon as the ball was snapped he unloaded on Troy. This always made Troy mad and he attacked which, I think was what Alvin wanted. He enjoyed irritating Troy. All three of the boys were good in football. Alvin hit "like a truck" was the words I heard other parents use describing his play. Nobody could get past Bo. He grabbed them because he read defenses so well. However at only 140 to 145, pounds sometime they could drag him but he never gave up. Troy hit like Alvin and was about the same size. Alvin set a record for most tackles in a season his senior year. Troy obliterated it his sophomore season.

Bo was probably the most durable of the three. Once after the play was over he ran back into the huddle yelling for Alvin to "pull it back, pull it back". Alvin had no idea what Bo wanted until Bo held out his hand and he saw some of Bo's fingers were not nearly normal in length. They had slipped back upon the top of his hand. Alvin grasped and pulled them with a jerk and they broke the huddle for the next play. Bo never left the game. Troy was far more laid back than the other boys. When in elementary school one spring he was going to play baseball. Saturday morning I woke him in time for him to make it to practice. He wasn't quite ready to get up and said "They don't have any business having practice on Saturday. I'm not going." Thus ended what would have never been an illustrious baseball career.

Troy was four years younger than Bo and in elementary until Bo was a Junior and Alvin a Senior. I would tell Troy that he was going to be better than his brothers in football as a means of trying to encourage him to play. When he reached junior high Mary said to me that maybe Troy didn't want to play football. I had never given that idea a single thought so one day I sat down with him reminding him of what I had told him for a few years. I said, "Son, that was Dad talking. I only want you to play football if that is what you want to do". He responded by telling me how much he wanted to play and then proved it on the field. As a seventh grader on one play alone he turned a huge loss into a fifteen yard gain by pancaking three defenders.

After the game one of my class mates from high school came up to me and said "Your boy cleaned house on that one play. He creamed a bunch of them."

Intimidation

Most everyone experiences intimidation of some form during their life. When I was a boy Dad started the Free Will Baptist Church in Lima, Ohio. The Lima church joined the Floyd County Conference in Kentucky since Dad had been licensed and later ordained in this Conference. Though I was quite young and was unaware of the workings of a Conference at the time I knew enough that I realized there were certain people who ran the Conference. I never knew these men were leaders and not "bosses", that they were elected by the people from the various churches that comprised the Conference. There was a preacher named Carl Senters who served the Conference. I had listened to men Dad's age talk about how strict and stern he was. I don't know that ever I spoke to him but I was intimidated by him. To me he represented firm solid Christian leadership. A no nonsense, either it's right or it's wrong kind of preacher. I held him in the highest of esteem even though I was not saved as yet. I never wanted this man to ever know that I had done or would do anything wrong. The world today needs more people, especially Christian leaders who exude what I always felt came from Brother Senters. We should live our lives so others can see Godliness in us. At no time should we ever try to make someone feel inferior to us. We should be examples of humility. Christians are simply sinners who have accepted Jesus gift of forgiveness. Brother Senters may have been a person who loved a good laugh, a clean joke, a lot of good clean fun. I never knew him personally. I knew enough that he was a person who stood on God's Word and was unwavering. This is what Jesus wants.

We should never intentionally attempt to intimidate another person. If we are intimidating to anyone it should be in the same manner I was by Brother Senters. May others feel toward us that we are surely what we profess, stand on what is right all the time, being unashamed to witness for our Lord. As Peter wrote that we should always be ready to give an answer to people of the hope that lies within us.

Each of us are no better than anyone else. As the founding fathers in America stated, "All men are created equal". Knowing this should help to keep us giving consideration to others.

Humility

Micah Chapter six, verse eight reads "He hath shewed thee, O man, what is good; and what doth the Lord require of thee, but to do justly, and to love mercy, and to walk humbly with thy God?"

This tells us that God requires three things from us.

Do justly, the right thing, the will of our Creator should be first and foremost in the hearts of every person on earth. This is God's will as much as anything else He gives us as instructions.

Love mercy, appreciate God's kindness given to mankind. Some folks cannot allow themselves to be thankful and happy for some other persons good fortune. Growing up I continually was told two things, be kind to others because they may be going through a trial or hard time that no one knows about, and to "Comfort the feeble minded". I almost always knew that when Mom said the latter that someone had done something she disagreed with or something absurd. Those words seemed to be her way of laughing it off.

The greatest mercy we can have has been given by God. He wants us to keep the golden rule by doing unto others as we would have others do unto us. If we can't be merciful to others why should we ever expect mercy from God.

Before moving to Ohio I spent most of the time playing with my cousin, Paul Vernon Conley. His parents lived in Number Five Camp at Lackey, KY. We lived on past Number Five at a house in the holler. There was another family living in Number Five named Taylor. They were a large family and one son was the age of Paul Vernon and myself. For some reason Paul didn't like this kid and though I never knew why when I was with Paul I went along with him because we were close buddies. One time Mom made some homemade chocolate candy (we never knew it was fudge until we had lived in Ohio several years) and I walked to Paul Vernon's taking some of the candy. We were enjoying the candy when the Taylor boy came over and asked for some. I would have given him some but Paul Vernon said no. Then Paul teased him with it. The boy left and Paul and I played until time for me to return home so we both went to my house. We met the Taylor boy coming from my house about a quarter mile away. He had some of the candy and told us he had told Mom that we wouldn't give him any but she did. I do not remember if I got in trouble with Mom that time but I assume I did. Something happened a few weeks later that made this incident sear into my brain and made me so sorry for not giving him candy that day. I was at Paul Vernon's one day and across the road at the Taylor house were two County Sheriff cars. I asked why and was told they came to take all the Taylor children away from their parents. I had no idea of the kind of home life those kids had but it had to have been sad for the authorities to take that action. Still today I am ashamed of my actions refusing to give that boy some candy. I can't even remember his first name but what I did I will always regret. I know God forgave me and if I knew where that boy was today I would contact him and ask forgiveness and personally make him a double batch of fudge. It would not be as good as what Mom made but I would add the same amount of peanut butter candy which is far better than Mom's recipe for it.

Walk humbly we are told because we are grateful. We are grateful because God gave us something we would never have in any way been able to provide for ourselves, the forgiveness of our sins.

Some Christians are like many people feeling they are better than others. Christians are actually no better than those who are not Christians. God loves us all equally and wants all to serve Him and Christians have accepted what Jesus did at Calvary. Since we had no hand in God's plan of salvation we should be so very thankful for what He instilled in our hearts when we came to him. Toward those who haven't turned their lives over to Jesus we should be very much concerned about their spiritual welfare desiring them to be saved also. We should never be arrogant in any way live humbly in their presence showing them we do sincerely care for them and the welfare of their souls.

If you noticed the last phrase of verse eight says "..... with thy God". Being humble is easy when walking with God. The Book of Hebrews recorded of Enoch being translated telling us that before his translation he left this testimony, that he pleased God. I know that pleasing God should be the primary goal of each person serving Him.

Humility is exhibited in the Bible several times, but never more than Jesus last hours prior to being crucified.

David by refusing to kill King Saul when the opportunity was presented saying, "God forbid that I should touch the Lord's anointed".

Stephen at his death by stoning prayed for God to "..... lay not this sin to their charge".

Tradition says that Peter was crucified upside down upon requesting it, feeling he was not worthy to die in the same manner as his Lord.

Humility and love go hand in hand and humility is best shown by love. Sometimes we lose our grasp on humility temporarily and when realizing it take hold of it again.

Mac Davis, the singer sang the words "Oh Lord it's hard to be humble when you're perfect in every way", which in reality is not possible.

Looking down on others is losing our grip on humility. I read of a couple who were having problems in their marriage to the point she was always belittling him. Both knew they needed some adjustments so they went to a fancy restaurant hoping to rekindle some of the lost spark. While there she told him there was a woman at the bar who couldn't take her eyes off him. He glanced at the woman and told his wife she had nothing to worry about because it was his first wife. Adding "I understand she has been drunk ever since we divorced". His wife's response was "It's hard to believe someone could celebrate continually for fifteen straight years". Her grasp was completely gone.

Referees

Referees are people too. Most sports fans don't seem to think so. I never wanted to be a referee. I found out when I had my leg broken that I'm not really into pain. There has to be a great deal of pain in the life of a referee or an umpire. When I was in the Air Force one day I was asked to umpire a softball game between two working sections of my squadron. The one section I remember was Overhead the other I know was either Dog Flight or Charlie Flight. I didn't ask why they wanted me to be the Ump just agreed to do it. One of the calls I made from behind the plate Sergeant Palmer, the First Sergeant, disagreed with and let me know in choice words. My reply was, "We're not in the Orderly Room now Sarge. There you are the boss. Here I'm the boss. What I say goes." That was the end of the discussion. I'm glad I wasn't up for promotion at the time. But I think Sergeant Palmer wasn't the kind of man that would let those words influence him in the promotion process. In the 1980s, I think, I read an article possibly in TV Guide about how tough talk on the football field just passes in the night as part of the game. One of the Oakland Raiders players told a member of the opposing team that after the game he was going to follow him to the parking lot and kill his family in front of him. Later admitting he was instantly wishing he had not said it. Afterward saying that he had probably been around (Lyle) Alzado too long. Some of the things spoken on the field and court during the process of the game can get rough. Compared to what I've heard said to referees it's not all that bad.

Troy started Varsity football all four years of high school. He was competitive, knew what each play was and how to carry out every players assignment, in case they forgot he told them what to do, and was as strong as anyone on the team. Troy always thought his dad could do anything and never let anyone do him or his friends wrong. One play stands out in my mind. It was an offensive passing play. The ball was thrown way off target and the receiver saw that it was going to a defensive player. The receiver runs over and pushes the defensive back out of the way and catches the ball which obviously is offensive pass interference. A flag is thrown. The referees talk among themselves for nearly fifteen minutes then give the ball to the other team. The crowd goes nuts. Troy leaves the huddle goes up to one referee and makes a profound statement. I'm shocked when he tells me at home after the game what he said. I quote him. "Mr. Referee, Sir, if that call costs us this game my Dad will kick your butt".

We have a group visit our church occasionally to sing for us once in a while, revivals, etc., called The Glory Way Quartet. Kevin Lyons from Marion, Ohio sings tenor. He has such a magnificent voice I am unable to describe how good he really is. Kevin, I found out, is also a referee. He has officiated games at Upper Scioto Valley our local school. Upper fans it has been said will kill you over a basketball game. One time during a service when he was singing with their group I told the church he was a referee and this was probably the first time he ever came to McGuffey without getting booed.

Once at a basketball game during a time out a referee was standing within arms' length of me. I and many others cheering for Upper Scioto valley were well aware the officials had missed numerous calls thus far. I removed my glasses reaching toward the referee telling him, "Hey Ref, take my glasses you're missing a great game out there". I did it without thinking and as usual when I do something stupid wished I had kept quiet. Over time I have managed to keep a lid on my trap much better. I'm still competitive when cheering for our Grandkids. Bo's oldest daughter, Lynsey is a great athlete. Watching her this past basketball season she drove to the basket and was mugged. Sitting in the top row of the bleachers the slaps could be heard even as hard of hearing as I presently am. The officials made no call on her drive. Immediately going on defense she was called for a foul, probably a good call, and instantly I'm thinking "How can all three officials miss a mugging like she took on that drive and then call a touch foul on her seconds later?

It seems that referees are the enemy. If our fans aren't upset with them the other teams fans are. They simply can't win for losing, can they? My advice to referees: "You need Jesus on your side."

The American Flag
And Our National Anthem

"Old Glory" has been for many years a definitive name for the American Flag. Most of us remember the television series "MASH" which ran many years and went into syndication even before finishing in prime time. In one episode Frank Burns says "Every morning when that flag goes up the pole I go with it." The line got a laugh without hardly anyone who wasn't a veteran of the military not giving it much thought. I've never went up the flag pole although I do relate to Frank's statement. We American Veterans take a great deal of pride in "Old Glory". Our hearts are lifted when we see her wave at an outdoor sporting event, inside a gymnasium hanging on the wall or as many now do, lower it from the ceiling for the singing of the National Anthem. When the anthem is sung I think all eyes should be on the flag and every person's right hand should be over their heart. This should be every person in the stadium or wherever the event is taking place including the participating athletes. This is not done by the majority of people present and it "grinds my gears" somewhat. It irritates me, disappoints me, makes me sad, and causes me to bite my tongue to keep from expressing my disgust to those failing to properly honor America. I think of myself as being in many ways a traditionalist. I certainly prefer the Christian hymns from my youth to what is called Contemporary Christian or Christian Rock. Also I prefer our National Anthem be sung in the traditional manner. Having retired from Wilson Sporting Goods I had opportunities while working to go with Wilson to different Super Bowls some of which I declined for personal reasons. I have watched most of the Super Bowl games since the days of the "Steel Curtain". A few I had no interest in because of who was playing. One of those was when Baltimore Ravens won. I'm not nor probably never will be one of their fans. I have no recollection of who sang the National Anthem at that game. One of the things I have noticed and have been very disappointed by is that too often whomever sings our Anthem before Super Bowls and College Championship contests do their own version instead of singing to honor America. I feel this diminishes our reverence for America. This bothered me enough that I wrote a letter to the NFL Commissioner Roger Goodell asking him to consider having people who perform at various high schools who sing the song properly according to tradition and from the heart. In my letter I even made recommendation of the best person I personally have heard perform. A very distinguished gentleman named Norman Cassidy who sings at Mohawk High School where our son Bo teaches and coaches. I realize the possibility of this happening is somewhere between slim and none but the Commissioner knows how I and many other patriots feel.

Flag Folding Ceremony

The flag folding ceremony described by the Uniformed Services is a dramatic and uplifting way to honor the flag on special days, like Memorial Day or Veterans Day, and is sometimes used at retirement ceremonies, and funerals.

The flag folding ceremony represents the same religious principles on which our country was originally founded. The portion of the flag denoting honor is the canton of blue containing the stars representing the states our veterans served in uniform. The canton field of blue dresses from left to right and is inverted when draped as a pall on a casket of a veteran who has served our country in uniform. In the Armed Forces of the United States, at the ceremony of retreat the flag is lowered, folded in a triangle fold and kept under watch throughout the night as a tribute to our nation's honored dead. The next morning it is brought out and, at the ceremony of reveille, run aloft as a symbol of our belief in the resurrection of the body.

Each fold represents something in particular.

The first fold of our flag is a symbol of life.

The second fold is a symbol of our belief in the eternal life.

The third fold is made in honor and remembrance of the veteran departing our ranks who gave a portion of life for the defense of our country to attain a peace throughout the world.

The fourth fold represents our weaker nature, for as American citizens trusting in God, it is to Him we turn in times of peace as well as in times of war for His divine guidance.

The fifth fold is a tribute to our country, for in the words of Stephen Decatur, "Our country, in dealing with other countries, may she always be right; but it is still our country, right or wrong."

The sixth fold is for where our hearts lie. It is with our heart that we pledge allegiance to the flag of the United States of America, and to the republic for which it stands, one nation, under God, indivisible, with liberty and justice for all.

The seventh fold is a tribute to our Armed Forces, for it is through the Armed Forces that we protect our country and our flag against all her enemies, whether they be found within or without the boundaries of our republic.

The eighth fold is a tribute to the one who entered in to the valley of the shadow of death, that we might see the light of day, and to honor mother, for whom it flies on mother's day.

The ninth fold is a tribute to womanhood; for it has been through their faith, love, loyalty and devotion that the character of the men and women who have made this country great have been molded.

The tenth fold is a tribute to father, for he, too, has given his sons and daughters for the defense of our country since they were first born.

The eleventh fold, in the eyes of a Hebrew citizen, represents the lower portion of the seal of King David and King Solomon, and glorifies, in their eyes, the God of Abraham, Isaac, and Jacob.

The twelfth fold, in the eyes of a Christian citizen, represents an emblem of eternity and glorifies, in their eyes, God the Father, the Son, and Holy Ghost.

When the flag is completely folded, the stars are uppermost, reminding us of our national motto, "In God we Trust." After the flag is completely folded and tucked in, it takes on the appearance of a cocked hat, ever reminding us of the soldiers who served under General George Washington and the sailors and marines who served under Captain John Paul Jones who were followed by their comrades and shipmates in the Armed Forces of the United States, preserving for us the rights, privileges, and freedoms we enjoy today.

(The Flag Folding Ceremony is from US Air Force website)

Nicknames

Why are nicknames given and what are the purposes? My best pal all through high school stuck me with a moniker which I hated but learned to accept. The way he came up with it was one Sunday afternoon he was at our house and though I don't recall what I said to irritate my oldest sister, Karen but she answered with "OK Toots". Emmett heard it and said "That's a good name for you". The next day at school he starts telling everybody to call me "Toots". I soon saw I couldn't stop it so I submitted and hoped that eventually folks would forget about it. After four years in the military some had forgotten. Now it has been fifty-one years since I was dubbed and still a few call me that and I immediately correct them. My barber was in our high school class and when I visit his shop he welcomes me by "Toots" if no one else is present. I correct him and we laugh. While I was in the Air Force I saw the movie "Splendor in the grass" and there was a character with that name played by Gary Lockwood. Believe me when I say I never told anyone about Toots Trusty while in the military.

I have never called Mary by a nickname. Since we have become grandparents I call her Grandma. The reason is I have never met anyone who enjoys being a grandma more that she does. I don't consider this a nickname. Some have nicknames that that seem to fit just right, some don't fit at all , and some don't have or need one. I'm sharing mine; but, don't you dare tell anyone. I was born in Lackey, Kentucky on December 19, 1944. Gee I'm old. When I was introduced to my older sister she, so I was told, (I was too young to remember) called me "Cutie". Many of the folks in Lackey called me by that one even when I was a teen visiting Dad's parents in the summer. Then in 1969, I went to the church in Lackey where my parents were saved. On Saturday we went to Mary Collins store there in Lackey where I always enjoyed going as a kid. Mary Collins daughter-in-law Beulah had worked there about as far back as I could remember. With me on that Saturday afternoon was the group my sister, Karen sang with. When we went into the store for a pop Beulah was there and looked at me and said "Is that you, Cutie?" Dean Brewer from the quartet absorbed what Beulah called me. When we left the store he said "Brother Cutie is gonna preach for us tonight". I asked him to keep that a secret. He never mentioned it to me again. Thank you Dean. I never understood why anyone would call me Cutie because my mother always told me and others in the family that I was the ugliest baby she ever saw. "He was all head, hands, and feet," she said. Also I was bald for my first six months.

Good Food

I have only met one person in my life who told me that he did not like to eat. To me that doesn't seem normal. I heard that some people eat to live and some live to eat. I have to be feeling pretty bad to not want to share in good eats. I don't have the appetite I used to but still enjoy good food. Mary is my favorite cook in the world. There have been some better such as Sylvia Bradley, Anvie Coburn, and when it comes to chicken and dumplings my mother. My personal favorite meal is soup beans and corn bread. Sometimes a few fried potatoes with them. And of course a good breath building sweet onion. The boys love Mary's cooking. So do the grandkids. Now the bomb. We were married for twenty-five years before I knew she didn't like to cook. My Uncle Troy was visiting and they were talking about cooking when she told him she didn't like to cook. I was stunned and told her how good she was at it and had never mentioned this before. Some things you do because they need to be done not because you like doing them. I think she enjoys it sometime especially when she knows the grand children are coming. She always wants to make something special for those occasions.

Free Will Baptists have churches which voluntarily unite and form Conferences which are good if a church needs assistance of some sort. They are great for fellowship among the members of the various churches. And a fringe benefit is the meals the host churches serve. There is usually fried chicken and most of the ladies from each church prepare some of the things they cook best. It's really good food. This tops off the really good things about the sessions of Conference being able to eat good food while talking to folks from the other churches that you don't get to see often.

My mother made the best apple pie ever. I never cared for apple pie as a child. By the time I was in my thirties my mind and taste buds definitely changed. She only used Jonathon or MacIntosh apples which cooked up to being so tasty. She used cinnamon in the apples which added to the taste. Everybody loved her apple pies. When I was growing up often on Friday Mom would make between sixteen and nineteen pies of different flavors. Apple was always included along with vanilla, chocolate, coconut, lemon, and butterscotch. She usually knew we would be having company the weekends she made a large number of pies. Almost always on Sunday evening there would not be a single piece of pie left.

One Sunday before Dad died there was supposed to be large crowd of people from the Willard, Ohio area come to the Lima church. Mom had cooked Friday and Saturday preparing to feed them. I never knew why but they never showed up. Dad announced to the people there that Mom had fixed so much to feed the visitors that didn't come so "I'm inviting everyone here to come to our house for Sunday dinner". When I heard Dad say that the first thought to go through my mind was, "Wait 'til Mom gets you off to yourself". Whether she ever mentioned anything to Dad or not I never knew. I do know that nearly all those at church that Sunday came to our house for dinner.

I just used the word "dinner". When we lived in Kentucky before moving to Ohio, the meal times were breakfast, dinner, and supper. We moved north and folks called them breakfast, lunch, and dinner. I still prefer the Kentucky version and usually speak of dinner in the middle of the day and supper in the evening. Call them however you wish; but, call me when it's ready.

Break A Leg

Let me say if there is any way you can avoid breaking anything go that direction. I had my leg broken at a high school football game November first 2002. It wasn't any fun at all. It was a freak accident. For two seasons I stood on the sidelines and took pictures for Bo's school football team. He would post team on the school's web site. The first playoff game, less than thirty seconds to go, I had put my camera in its bag, standing behind the team talking to someone facing away from the field. Hearing a noise behind me I saw the team separating and one of Bo's players tackled one of the other team members. The tackle was near the out of bounds line and came sliding in my direction. My instinct was to go to the right but the man I was talking to was on my right so I shifted to my left foot and before I could move they had slid into me. If I had went down I would only have been bruised or maybe only a little sore. But I didn't want to be embarrassed by getting knocked down in front of the huge crowd. So I leaned back to stay upright while trying to free one of my feet. The inertia from their momentum had both feet trapped. I felt my right femur bend and then snap. Now I had no problem going down.

As a result I spent from November first until November twenty-six in the hospital. during this time I had lots of visitors. Some from various churches along with numerous friends and people from the shop where I worked. Chuck and Sharon (J.B.) Fisher came to see me and were shocked to find me with a tube through my nose to my stomach to drain its contents so my stomach would heal. I had been given liquid potassium to drink and even though diluted with apple juice it was the most awful taste I have ever encountered. Sharon thought I was nearly done for after seeing me. If you have never had a tube down your throat be thankful. If you try to speak it gags you which can cause the tube to come up when you don't want it to. If this happens the tube is pulled completely out and a new one is reinserted up your nose then down the back of your throat into the stomach. It isn't pleasant.

Jackie O. came to see me. Not the former first lady but a much nicer one.

Friends Jim and Michelle Burkett visited and it was a real pick me up when I really needed one. Both Mary and I feel they are special people and have great respect for them.

During the next nine months I learned a lot of things. The first being if someone tells you to "Break a leg" don't do it. There are too many problems that will follow. A few are arthritis, after and even during the healing process, wheelchairs, walkers, pain and discomfort, surgery to repair the break, lower back pain from your hips no longer being level because the bad leg is now significantly shorter than it was. I am well aware that the phrase "Break a leg" is used to try to motivate people to give their best efforts. In that perspective when it comes to the Lord's work we should recall Paul's writing to the Philippians in chapter three, verses 13, and 14. *Brethren, I count not myself to have apprehended: but this one thing I do, forgetting those things which are behind, and reaching forth unto those things which are before, I press toward the mark for the prize of the high calling of God in Christ Jesus.* This is when it's really all right to "Break a leg". Give to Him all you have in effort.

Don't Let The Parrot
Be The One
To Bring You To Your Knees

Mary's dad, Zack Standifer, had a parrot. It was cute but I don't want one. Before Papa Zack got the parrot his oldest son John had one. Mary I went for a visit at John's in North Judson, Indiana in the late 1960s. John took me to the back bedroom to show me his parrot. I remember it had a lot of green and small parts of yellow. It also stood on one foot while holding a saltine cracker in the other foot which he would occasionally raise to take a bite of the cracker. While seeing the parrot I noticed the dresser and chest of drawers had most of their drawers opened a little bit. The corners of the drawers were rounded and/or splintered. I asked John what in the world had happened to the bedroom suit. He pointed out the door on the bird cage being open. I then noticed the cage was well more than three feet tall to accommodate the large bird. John said he left the drawers partially opened so the parrot could sharpen his beak. That short conversation convinced me I don't ever want a parrot. Back to Zack's parrot. We were visiting once and most of Mary's relatives who lived in the Salyersville area came to Zack's while we were there. Zack would pop some popcorn for his parrot, sometimes placing a few kernels in his palm and extending it inside the cage. The parrot would eat them one at a time. Sometimes Zack would take a single kernel picking it up with his index finger and thumb which he then would hold close to the cage. The parrot would stick his head between the bars of the cage and gently take the kernel in his beak and eat it then want more. Mary's youngest brother, Charles decided he would feed the parrot in this manner. Mr. parrot extended his head through the bars gently taking the popped kernel in his beak and eating it just as it did for Zack. After accepting a few kernels from Charlie Mr. Parrot reached his head out for another kernel which Charlie was pleased to give. Mr. Parrot gently opens his mouth for the kernel then without any indication of his intentions turned his head slightly and clamped down upon Charlie's finger. I had been told previous to that time that parrots had a powerful bite from the great strength in their beaks, jaws, or wherever. Remembering John's bedroom suit I certainly believed it. Charlie affirmed that fact on that particular evening. I'm unsure if I can properly or adequately describe the scene that followed. If preachers could get the same reaction after a sermon, and altar invitations would be responded to in this manner, revival would spring up all across America. Mr. Parrott grasps Charlie's finger, Charlie immediately felt something, his mind tells him what he feels is pain, he jerks to withdraw from the bird's beak. The grip of the beak is tremendously strong and Charlie cannot break it. Immediately he falls to his knees. He is now begging the bird to release him. "Let go parrot, please let loose, somebody help me, please parrot." I don't think the parrot had nearly as good a grasp of English as he did Charlie's finger. This parrot was like the devil holding on to a sinner. He doesn't want to give him up. Charlie is now on his knees begging and pleading for release. If old time conviction through the power of the Holy Spirit were to grasp people's hearts in this manner we could have a wonderful growth in the numbers of people entering the Kingdom of God. When the Holy Spirit grabs your heart again drawing you to Christ remember Papa Zack's parrot. This grasp may cause panic for a while but surrender to Jesus and the pain goes away. Don't wait for the parrot to bring you to your knees.

Hard-Shells, Holy Rollers And Hypocrites

Having encountered each of these in over more than forty-five years in ministry I feel it would be a shortcoming on my part to not speak of them.

Hard-shells

To avoid embarrassment to relatives of this individual I omit his name. I was quite well acquainted with someone who was a Hard-shell Baptist preacher. For those who are unfamiliar with the term Hard-shell I will explain. They are so strongly set in their traditions and beliefs it is nearly impossible to change their mind about any ideas and concepts they hold. I can see where it is a good thing to have a hard shell, like a turtle, so as not to be easily offended and having the spiritual stamina to endure some unpleasant things Christians face. The preacher I refer to felt members of his denomination was the only ones who would get to go to Heaven. I spent some time at his home and observed him to be friendly with folks from his church. However if ever he gave a kind word to a child it had to have been out of my hearing. He was grouchy to me every time I was visiting that home. Though a lad myself I never heard him say anything nice to his wife who was always glad to see any child come there to visit. She went out of her way for any kids. I actually felt sorry for her at times observing what I considered mistreatment of her. Probably not all Hard-shell people are like this man was. My Mother's parents belonged to a church considered to be Hard-shell Baptist. When we first moved to Ohio we stayed with them a few weeks. Mom and Dad went to their church a time or two but Grandpa would take the pulpit and degrade those who were not of their "faith and order". I don't remember those visits probably because I usually napped through the preaching part of church services. After I was grown Mom told me of this and other things. She told me that once Grandpa told her that she and Dad had not even been baptized properly because they weren't baptized in his "faith and order". Hard-shells would not allow other denominations to participate in communion services with them. I always felt what this said to other Christians was, "You are not as good as we are. You aren't good enough to partake with us." Reminded me of the early New Testament Church when some did not want to accept Gentiles or to fellowship with them. Also in their services musical instruments were forbidden. Even after reading Psalm 150, they stuck with their belief.

Holy Rollers

I first heard this title as a small boy with it being applied to Charismatic's, those we used to refer to as Pentecostals. By using this label I hope to offend no one. That would never be my intent. When I was a child there was a church in my home town that was handling snakes. This is what many of the kids here were told. I was curious as to whether this was true. However, I was too chicken to go to one of their services. After all, if I went and a snake got loose someone may be bitten and definitely this was never going to happen to me, because I'm not stupid enough to get around it. I have read in depth of these folks who practice this and for the life of me don't know why they would believe much less practice this.

Scott Clemons, a dear friend who passed on around twenty years ago, told me of when he was a young man living in Kentucky something I will share. Scott and his friend Jim, were working in a field and one came across a rattle snake. They cut a limb from a tree with a fork in it and pinned the snake's head to the ground. Now they decided one would hold the snake like this so he couldn't get away while the other went to the house and made a box to put it in. The box was a frame of wood with screen wire covering all sides including the door on top. Also, they attached several feet of rope to each end of the box so they would each be at a safe distance in case the viper escaped the box. Jim asked Scott what he intended to do with the snake. "I'm gonna take him over to the Pentecostal church and watch him eat that preacher alive." I don't think that I need to point out that this was years before Scott got saved. That evening Jim and Scott carried their box into the church yard. The preacher asked Scott what was in the box. Scott told him "A rattler with twenty-one rattles and a button". "What are you going to do with him?", asked the preacher. Scott says "I'm gonna let him out and shoot him right here in the church yard." Preacher: "Don't do that Scott. Let me have him." Scott: "Okay, you can have him if you take him into church and handle him. If he bites anybody I'll shoot him right then." Scott and Jim enter the church and sit on the front pew. The box is carried in and placed on the altar in front to Scott. The service starts and the preacher is sitting in a chair against the wall several feet from the box. After awhile the preacher gets up, walks over to the box, waves his hand over the top screen. Mr. Rattler hits the inside of the screen with his head evidently going after the preacher's hand. The preacher turned pale and returned to his chair. After awhile he rises and comes before the box again. He again waves his hand over the top screen and there is no response from inside. He unlocks the lid and starts to open it. Scott said that now he and Jim were standing in their seat with hands on their pistols. The preacher has the lid all the way up and reaches in for Mr. Rattler. Scott told me "I knowed that was one dead preacher". Scott was wrong. He said the preacher picked up Mr. Rattler, carried him around, wrapped him around his neck, stroked him and carried him all over the church. After several minutes of this he returned him to the box closed the lid and then picked up the box and placed it against the wall behind the pulpit. After church was ended Scott said he told the preacher he brought the snake just to watch him eat the preacher. Since the preacher handled him he now belonged to the preacher. The preacher told Scott that this snake would have a great future by travelling to New York and other places. It was enjoyable for me when Scott related this event to me but it did nothing to improve my feelings about snakes.

They always did give me the creeps. In scripture they represent the devil. You can never trust him. He is deceitful, cunning, and always searching for someone to take advantage of which will result in their ruin. I went to a few Pentecostal churches as a kid. Some of the things they did I did not understand. At that time I shrugged it off and never gave it serious thought. After my military service I spent untold hours studying their doctrine. My mindset was if they have something I need or should have I want it. If their belief and doctrine is supported by scripture I'll jump on board.

As I said earlier I am a Free Will Baptist. We do not agree with Charismatics on receiving the Holy Spirit after being saved because of "Ephesians 1:13, In whom ye also trusted, after that ye heard the word of truth, the gospel of your salvation: in whom also after that ye believed, ye were sealed with that holy Spirit of promise, 14, Which is the earnest of our inheritance until the redemption of the purchased possession, unto the praise of his glory." Paul writes nothing about seeking the Holy Spirit after being saved. On the day of Pentecost they were waiting for the Holy Spirit. The late Dr. George E. Gardiner wrote "The Corinthian Catastrophe" and explains the scriptures of most Charismatic doctrines as well as anyone I have ever read. He was raised inside the movement and had numerous questions which intense and deep study made plain to him. I heartily recommend this book. It is approximately sixty-two pages in length.

Hypocrites

Jesus faced and dealt with these types while He was here on Earth. They have always been around the church. They are a tremendous hindrance to unsaved people coming to Jesus. If you have been a Christian for any length of time most likely you have encountered some also. Hypocrites come in various shapes and sizes. The problem is you can't pick them out just by looking the crowd over. If that were possible it would certainly save us a great deal of time, trouble, and heart ache. Jesus spoke to the Pharisees and other groups calling them what they were. He had an insight that we don't for He looked upon the heart. Our recognition of them comes over time. When but sixteen years of age I heard a man preach at a revival in the Wabash, Indiana area and was impressed. I never saw him again for more than a decade when he came to a church in our area for revival. I remembered him and attended that revival. I did not know why but there was an uneasy feeling that I had about him. What he spoke from the pulpit was the Bible and he was accepted by nearly all who heard him. He had a winning personality accompanied by intelligence and knowledge of scripture but I couldn't shake that feeling of uneasiness. It took over a year and a half before I realized why I had that particular feeling. In conversation he told me something and more than six months later on the same subject he told me something completely different. I then knew he wasn't what he professed. As time went by other people from other churches, some of which were in different states, would bring up this man in conversations. They told me almost exactly the same stories of how he would elicit money from folks who could not afford to lose it, how he had a lady friend in Cincinnati, Ohio, whom he visited between revivals. He was a married man but for some reason his wife never travelled with him.

I know a woman whose husband was as dedicated a Christian as anyone I have met. She is deceitful, cannot be believed, stirs things up among fellow Christians, plays on peoples sympathy to get what she wants, cost a dear friend thousands of dollars he couldn't afford, and lied about it to the man's son when he confronted her about it. There are people who think she is a saint since she chooses her victims carefully leaving them unaware of her actions. Those like her are tremendously dangerous to the unwary. This woman's favorite preacher lied to me twice. What is it they say about "birds of a feather"? Scripture teaches if a brother walks disorderly to keep no company with them. See Phil 3:18 (For many walk, of whom I have told you often, and now tell you even weeping, that they are the enemies of the cross of Christ: 19 Whose end is destruction, whose God is their belly, and whose glory is in their shame, who mind earthly things.)

Some people just want their way in everything. This is only natural but we should give consideration to other individuals and what the end results can be. Often what can be if we have our way is really not what should be so we need to forego what we desire for what is best for God's work and will.

I've seen folks do some rather underhanded things just to get their way in a church where the end result usually nowhere near what was best for His kingdom.

Shall We Pray?

In the early 1950s, my Dad along with Melvin Staggs and Wick Howard saw a need to have a Free Will Baptist Conference that would include the church Dad founded in Lima and the Claypool and Wabash, Indiana churches. The representatives of the three churches met and agreed to form a Conference. Since all were familiar with the Floyd County Conference in Kentucky and Dad had led the Lima Church to unite with them they asked for Floyd County to send a committee to preside over the Organizational Meeting.

There were five or six men who came from Floyd County to Wabash to take care of this business. The three churches forming the new Conference chose to name it the Kosciusko County Conference. The Conference still exists and has grown tremendously. In October of 2004, they celebrated their fiftieth anniversary. I was invited to come for a presentation on behalf of my Dad. Dad was the first Moderator of the Conference elected at the initial meeting. They presented me with a large framed copy of the minutes of the Organizational Meeting, which hangs on the wall in my office at home, and a picture of Mom and Dad. It was a time of good fellowship for me as I saw many friends I had made during the years preaching in most all of the Conference's churches.

All I know about the meeting to organize the churches into a Conference has been passed down to me by older folks who were there. Brother Roy Burkhart told me of this more than once. The Committee from Floyd County was given expense money from the new Conference but on the return trip to their homes were stopped for speeding. Evidently the driver wasn't paying attention as he should have been and the police stopped them. There was a young man with the older preachers on the trip and when they were stopped he said, "We better pray about this", probably trying to be funny. Then Brother Carl Senters told him "It's too late to pray, now we have to pay".

Caught being guilty there could only be on conclusion. Now we have to pay. Stop to think that when Christ returns all living will be caught. We will be caught in our sins or in our living for the Saviour. There will then be heard something the guilty in sin won't wish to hear. "Depart......". Go, get away from Him, good-by forever more. It will then be too late to pray and time to pay.

Saying grace, ask the blessing, turn thanks are phrases for prayer before eating. Why do we do that? Most answer because we are thankful. And that is true as we should be thankful for all God gives us. But the primary reason is we ask God to bless our food because everything we consume in food comes directly or indirectly from the ground. The ground was cursed as part of the sentence imposed upon mankind because of Adam and Eve's transgression in the Garden of Eden. We ask God to bless what we eat and this eliminates the curse. The meat we enjoy comes indirectly from the ground in that it is nourished by what comes from the ground. The vegetables we love grow directly from the ground thereby bringing the need for the curse to be removed by asking the Almighty to bless it.

We kids had to take our turn at the supper table each evening when we were young. One day at school I learned a new prayer and used it that evening as it was my turn to pray before supper. I thought Dad would like it. We all bowed our heads and I prayed.... "Praise the Lord and the Holy Ghost, the one that eats the fastest gets the most." Opening my eyes after such a good prayer I expected to see a big grin on Dad's face. Man alive, did I ever get a letdown. Dad had a look that told me he wasn't pleased with what he heard. He looked me in the eye and told me I didn't deserve any supper to go straight to bed, right now.

I knew Dad had a sense of humor and thought he would laugh at my prayer. I never dreamed it would be such a disappointment to him.

Some times the things we say or do are disappointing to our Heavenly Father so we should always try to avoid that by giving thought to each thing we say and/or do.

Great Commercials

Bob Phillips has written numerous clean joke books containing much about church. One story tells of a young girl attending church for the very first time. The pastor, knowing this to be her first visit, asked her as she was leaving how she liked the service. She said she really liked the music part "but the commercial was too long". In essence preaching is a commercial about God's plan of salvation.

Television commercials are something most people would prefer did not exist. However there are some that remain in my memory not especially because of the product but as a result of what they made the boys say. When Alvin and Bo were young they would be running through the house playing and if going through the living room and the TV was showing a commercial they would stop in their tracks to watch it. After it finished they would resume playing as though the commercial left no impression.. There were a few that brought comments from them though. That was when I realized commercials were probably designed on a child's level. Maybe because this way they attracted more attention. A commercial for RidX that helps deteriorate sewage in septic tanks started with the words, "Imagine a volcano erupting on your front lawn" and ended with "Get RidX before trouble starts". After stopping to view this ad before starting to play again Alvin turns to me and says, "Dad we better get RidX before trouble starts". Troy always liked the one about a deodorizer. I don't remember the name of the product but Troy loved it. It started "The fish that came to dinner and stayed". The product could also to take care of the "damp musties and the Old Fogies Stogy". Troy recited these two from memory every time they came on.

One year a commercial aired at the Super Bowl which I liked. The product eludes me but it showed all these cowboys on horseback "herding cats". The next day when I arrived at work I told my supervisor I was giving my two week notice. I think he really thought I was quitting until I told him I was going to get a job herding cats.

The best commercial to me personally was during the NCAA basketball playoffs this year. It was for State Farm. Since I've been with State Farm for decades I usually watch their commercial if it is a new one. I was at the computer during a break in the action when I recognized a familiar voice. It was Coach Bobby Knight. I looked up the see the Agent shaking from fright as he told the Coach he should be happy with the money he saved with State Farm. Coach screams "Don't I look like I'm happy?" then turns to leave and after he steps outside all the other workers in the office climb from under desks and behind things where they were hiding. About that time Coach Knight sticks his head back inside and all the ones who had come from hiding dived again to get out of his sight. All the Coach said was "Thanks Again". Every time they aired this one I watched it in its entirety.

The only time I ever felt myself to be hypocritical was when I said that If I had been the best high school basketball player in the country I could never have played for Bobby Knight. But, if my son was the best in the country I would want him to play for Coach Knight.

Coach really didn't throw that chair out of anger. Speaking before a civic group later he said he saw a little old lady on the other side of the gymnasium having to stand to watch the game and he was just giving her his seat.

Does The Bible Mean What It Says?

The times in which we now live are fearful from the stand point of the questioning of and disregard for what was written under the inspiration of the Almighty. Some denominations have called into question God's plan and outline for marriage. Some have agreed that there is no sin in taking the life of an unborn baby. Numerous ones have not only accepted homosexuality as appropriate for being members of their churches but some have gone far enough to allow and accept them as pastors. *"For I am the Lord, I change not;"* says a portion of Mal 3:6. Lev 20:13 states *"If a man also lie with mankind, as he lieth with a woman, both of them have committed an abomination: they shall surely be put to death; their blood shall be upon them."* Both of the previous scriptures are from the Old Testament. Some say Leviticus is about the Law given to Moses which is no longer in effect today. The law was fulfilled and Paul said some parts of it were changed. The ceremonial and sacrificial portions were eliminated. In Heb 7:12 Paul writes *" For the priesthood being changed, there is made of necessity a change also of the law."* This changes being the doing away of the ceremonial and sacrificial portions of the law.

A family has a son who informs them he is "gay", a word I don't agree with as a definition of what the Bible says is sin. The son tells his family he didn't really want to be that way, that "God made him that way". The family accepts that and sees nothing wrong with the son living what scripture calls an abominable life. What does the Bible say about this? That son may believe what he said. He either does not know that God does **never** condemn something and then later tell an individual it isn't wrong for him or her. Read what the Creator said of everything he made in Gen 1:31 *And God saw everything that he had made, and, behold, it was very good. And the evening and the morning were the sixth day.* God made **no** junk. He never made anything that He later condemned. He condemns how we have changed and corrupted His created things.

Several years ago the United Methodist denomination held their national convention in Cleveland, Ohio. Their most published topic in the media was whether or not they were going to allow the ordination of practicing homosexual men and women. While reading this in the local newspaper during that week I was flabbergasted. I wondered if their leadership has reached the status where they know more and are more intelligent than He who created them. Have they reached the point of those addressed by the apostle in Rom 1:*21 Because that, when they knew God, they glorified him not as God, neither were thankful; but became vain in their imaginations, and their foolish heart was darkened. 22 Professing themselves to be wise, they became fools, 23 And changed the glory of the uncorruptible God into an image made like to corruptible man, and to birds, and fourfooted beasts, and creeping things. 24 Wherefore God also gave them up to uncleanness through the lusts of their own hearts, to dishonour their own bodies between themselves: 25 Who changed the truth of God into a lie, and worshipped and served the creature more than the Creator, who is blessed for ever. Amen.*

I since found out there is a faction of the United Methodist denomination that is pushing the homosexual agenda. Biblically this group of people should be dealt with. When writing to the church at Corinth the Apostle Paul confronted them about a man who had married his father's wife. He told them that even among the Gentiles who had no relationship with God would never let such a thing be permitted among themselves.

The denominations facing issues that the Bible is so specific about should expel all involved and declare to all the world that God is the one who set the standard and they will uphold it regardless.

My favorite preacher in my youth was Rev. Joe M. Wireman and often I recall having heard him say

"Sometimes we think we know more than God". That is an

impossibility, not that people would think that but we can never know more than Him. Our minds are finite and His is infinite. We are within certain limits while God is totally unlimited. All of our human powers, ideas, intentions, abilities, and even our possibilities are limited. God is limitless. He spoke and the universe came into being. Jesus told us we cannot add anything to the height of our own body. Since God made man common sense should make us reason that if He has the power to make us He then also has the power to destroy us if He wills it. Therefore we should have in our hearts a fear of Him. *"The fear of the Lord is the beginning of wisdom and the knowledge of the holy is understanding."* (Prov 9:10) Also Psalm 111:10, teaches this in part. If God's Word says it then it should be forever settled in our hearts how it is and always will be. People can be deceived and one of the best examples is Joseph Smith, Jr. He proclaimed to have seen and talked with God face to face when the Bible clearly tells us in John 1:18, that *"No man hath seen God at any time"*. Also from John 5:37, *And the Father himself, which hath sent me, hath borne witness of me. Ye have neither heard his voice at any time, nor seen his shape.* God's word never declares something wrong and elsewhere say it is alright.

Abortion is a subject many don't want mentioned. In America folks say it is the woman's right to choose. Certainly I agree with a woman's right to choose but differently than the law. I believe a woman has the right to choose whether she gets into a sexual relationship or not realizing the prospect it could cause pregnancy. If she chooses to take the risk and then discovers she is expecting her choices are over. You may have heard the one about three men discussing when life begins and one, like myself believes it begins at conception, one believes it begins at birth. The third gentleman informs them they are both wrong saying "Life begins after all the kids move out and the family dog dies" leaving no restrictions for the man and wife. Naturally there are adjustments to life after the kids all leave the nest. This time has some good parts and some bad parts.

Definitely life begins at conception. To prove it go the Bible Exodus 21:22-23 indicate that the aborting of a fetus was equivalent to the murdering of the child. The guilty party was punished as a murderer if the mother or the unborn child, or both, died. From Exodus 21:25 comes these words. The NIV quote is *"If men who are fighting hit a pregnant woman and she gives birth prematurely but there is no serious injury, the offender must be fined whatever the woman's husband demands and the court allows. But if there is serious injury, you are to take life for life, eye for eye, tooth for tooth, hand for hand, foot for foot, burn for burn, wound for wound, bruise for bruise."* If God is that protective of the unborn how dare anyone claim the right to choose abortion. The only logical reason I can think of for folks to go against what the Bible says is they think they are smarter than God. As Adam and Eve hid their nakedness with fig leaves after disobeying the Lord. The fig leaves represent self righteousness. We cover our sins and shortcomings. I caution to remember there will be a day when every secret thing will be uncovered.

Abortion is a big issue in American Politics. I prefer to avoid the risk of facing Jesus on judgment day and Him maybe asking the question "Why did you vote for someone who would approve killing unborn babies?" Murder will be punished. If I support a murderer the scripture teaches that makes me equally guilty. Revelation 20:12, tells us of God's record book. He is unlike us in that we sometimes forget. He never forgets anything except for our sins cast into the sea of forgetfulness. Matt 12:36, *But I say unto you, That every idle word that men shall speak, they shall give account thereof in the day of judgment. 37 For by thy words thou shalt be justified, and by thy words thou shalt be condemned.*

A vote from a person is a word that expresses either my rejecting or endorsing what the person stands for. Candidates may stand for things we don't care for and our voting for them be okay. However if they stand on any issue contrary to God's Word don't jeopardize your soul. I leave this with one question. What excuse will God accept?

Prejudice

What is prejudice? Unreasonable feelings, opinions, or attitudes, especially of a hostile nature, regarding a racial, religious, or national group. Since there are different types of prejudice I wish only to mention the above three.

Racial prejudice is something that should never exist. The reason being the same God who made one race of humans made all the other races. Being from Southeastern Kentucky as a lad I have no memory of seeing a black person when we lived there. However the folks there referred to blacks using the "N" word which we thought nothing about. Not being around them I had no idea that referring to them as such was offensive. The first time I ever saw a black person I was probably seven years of age. I was not shocked or stunned, neither was I fearful. I guess the best descriptive word would be curious. In the military I spent much time amid the black soldiers and treated them just like one of the other soldiers. I made some friends I've never forgotten. Willie Jones, whom we called "Cue" because he was the best I ever saw shoot pool. Charlie Davis was 8th Air Force judo champion. He and I would go to the Seven/Eleven store outside the main gate and buy a watermelon then halve it and eat it in the barracks. He would smack his lips and say "Mmmm-mm, sure is good ain't it Trus?". I got along with all the men regardless of race. One big reason was I was raised to treat people like I would want them to treat me. One of the sweetest and dearest Christians I know is Willie Campbell. He has been to our home attended and spoken at our church, loves Mary's cooking, and though he is black I don't think of Willie as a black man. I think of him as my brother. Once he and I were eating at Cracker Barrel and Willie told the waitress we were twins and the only difference in us was that I was a little younger than him. Willie's church honored him, and his wife Sue called to invite me as well as sending a card. Mary and I went and were treated super. I was asked to say something about Willie. Naturally I told them of we being twins. In Heaven there will be no segregation or separation of any type. If prejudice accomplishes anything at all it has to be that it will keep people from getting to Heaven. I remember Martin Luther King, Jr. in his speech from 1963, in Washington, D.C., when he spoke of his dream that one day his children would be judged "not by the color of their skin; but, by the content of their character". This is the Christian attitude.

Religious prejudice is difficult to understand on my part. I am well aware of religious cults like Jehovah's Witness, Mormon, those in communes, etc. For Bible-believing God-fearing denominations there is no need for prejudice. Some church members are prejudiced against larger or smaller churches. Some folks don't want any church to grow except the one to which they are a member. If Christ is preached and people believe and receive Christ all Christians everywhere should rejoice. The Bible tells us how to deal with those who walk disorderly as well as those teaching falsehoods. Prejudice of national groups as well as other groups is to me utterly silly. Democrats despise Republicans and vice versa. Some Southerners don't care for Northerners as well as the other way around. Army doesn't like Navy, soldiers on active duty have little if any respect for the reservists or National Guard, Marines don't like it because they are basically a part of the Navy. It goes even to the work place. Day shift doesn't care for the night shift. Night shift says day shift goofs off too much and don't work as hard as they do on nights. I surmise that most of this type of prejudice is too easily picked up by lots of folks. It shouldn't happen. Some just don't play well with others. We always want things one hundred per cent our way. Why? Because we are always right. If you don't see it my way then you are wrong. Shame on us. Reminds me of two pastors in the same town. Their churches are different denominations, therefore there is some doctrinal differences of which each is aware. Still they get together on occasion socially and they always spend some of that time talking about their churches. One day one let his prejudice show when he told the other, "We are both trying to do God's will, you in your way and me in God's way".

Why Such Variations Among Christians?

Different Christian denominations spawn from disagreements of doctrine, disagreements of practice, and quite likely from personality clashes. Some people want to be the boss, the leader, or the one being followed. Some think they should be at the top of the totem pole thinking this will cause others to respect and admire them. This should never enter the Christians mind. Though there exists the aforementioned differences there is one thing all Christians should always have in common. That common thing is there should be a certain standard which upholds obvious Christian teachings. The Bible says "Let God be true and every man a liar". If the Bible says it is sin then all Christians should agree that it is sin. This should never be challenged. Those challenging what God has spoken through the written Word should be dealt with as heretics or disobedient followers.

Because we have failed to collectively hold that standard the Church of the first born (Heb 12:23 To the general assembly and church of the firstborn, ...) has lost a great deal of its influence. The result of losing our influence can be seen all over America. The church should and could have a tremendous impact on many things if we stand behind what is Biblical and raise the standard as a flag raised high for the world to see if we have the back bone and gumption to do so. One or a few cannot have a great impact. I believe if everyone who claims Christ as Saviour would take a public stand we could accomplish things and have a significant impact from the Atlantic to the Pacific.

Here is an example, my all time favorite soft drink is Diet Mountain Dew. Scrumdiliumptious, mmmm good. I have not tasted one in over two and a half years. The reason is because it is made and marketed by Pepsico which is a conglomerate of businesses. Pepsico has given to gay rights organizations millions of dollars for several years. They also own Taco Bell, Pizza Hut, Quaker Oats, Gatorade, and numerous other businesses. I do not knowingly purchase anything they sell. If every person in America professing Christianity would boycott them it would have a major impact on their profits. There are numerous big businesses that do as Pepsico. Home Depot is another. We should avoid all dealings with them. Corporations look for the bottom line and if a third of their income is lost it will be addressed by their leadership.

My stand on this may be considered a "John the Baptist" one, (the voice of one crying in the wilderness). Can you imagine the impact Christianity could have in even the stock market if we quit supporting those who promote and sponsor sin?

Buckeyes And Hillbillies

I'm a Hillbilly that was transplanted in 1951, in Ohio. When we moved here I hated it. We arrived late Sunday night on Labor Day weekend. Monday was a holiday. School started Tuesday. Hate is not strong enough to express my feelings for that particular day. First off, I don't think any of the teachers wanted me. I got that impression when they led me to one of the second grade class rooms and the teacher, Mrs. Cummings, said she didn't want me. Why I don't know. To a kid seven years old hearing someone say "I don't want him", was disturbing. It might be a matter of seating room or something else. Whatever the reason I wasn't told. Nobody wants me here. They do in Lackey, Kentucky, though. My cousin Paul Vernon Conley I knew was missing me. How do I get back to good old Lackey? If I would have had any idea how to get back to Lackey I would have taken off walking to go back where I knew the other kids. I don't know anyone here. And they ain't friendly either. When that first day in a new school finished I came outside and Grandpa Conley was waiting to walk me back to his house. I didn't even know how to get back there. Let's go back to Lackey. Though being somewhat shy and feeling out of place I did make friends with some of the other kids. I learned the way to Grandpa and Granny Conley's. We stayed with them for a few weeks before Mom and Dad purchased a house. We had an upstairs in the house. We had made the big time. WOW!! Some days after school on the way home someone would say something about "them dumb Hillbillies". Them's fighting words, buddy. Win some and lose some, Lord, I hate it here. How do I get back to Lackey? I start to accept the fact that I can't go back to Lackey and make adjustments. I get along okay with about every person in the class; however I'm still a hillbilly. We don't like to be picked on or made fun of. Probably all people feel this way.

One day after school walking home one of the boys, Ron Donnal, jabbed or tapped me when he left Main Street to run a block west to his house. He was laughing as he ran away after nudging me. That didn't sit well with me. Looking around I saw a piece of a brick on the ground, picked it up, and threw it at him. Hit him solidly in the back. I can still recall the scream he let out. I showed him. Well, the next morning at school Ron's older brother Leonard come into our cloak room and informs me I am in BIG trouble. Their mother wrote a note to Mrs. Scott our teacher. I tell Ron that I would bring him a nickel to school the next day if he doesn't show Mrs. Scott the note. I think Ron was giving the idea some thought. Leonard speaks up and tells Ron not to do it. Ron would like to have the nickel. In 1951, and 1952, that was a lot of money. Ron makes the right choice. He gives the note to whom it was addressed. Talk about a miserable day in school that was as long as D-Day was for the troops going ashore in France. I know I'm going to get at least two whippings over that brick. One from the teacher the other from one of my parents. (If I get paddled at school I get another when they find it out.) Mrs. Scott waited until nearly the end of the day to handle the situation. If she would have whipped me early in the morning I would be over it by now. But no, she makes me worry all day. Two whippings in two hours is not appealing to any second grader. I apologize, eat crow and humble pie all simultaneously. Mrs. Scott was very nice. She talked firmly to both Ron and I and nobody got paddled. It was over and in a few minutes we could go home from school. What a day. Ron and I became friends and so with Leonard. Ron moved to Florida after we were grown and I haven't seen him in close to forty years. Leonard still lives here in town and is a dedicated Christian. Their parents, Arthur and Loretta lived in the same house until they sold out after he retired and moved to Florida. For years after military service we lived neighbors to them and could never wanted nicer neighbors. Now they have both gone to be with Jesus and I expect to meet them one day. Ron's mother acquired Alzheimer's eventually going to a home. Art came back to Ohio for a short last visit and I got to speak with him which was a pleasure.

As the years went by I only got to return to Lackey during summer vacation from school. I always remembered the old saying "You can take a boy out of the hills; but you can't take the hills out of a boy". After military service was completed I told people that no longer applied to me. I thought I would die when we first moved to Ohio. If now I had to move back to Lackey I know I would die. I visit there occasionally but it is no longer the same. Those of my youth moved away. Most I have no inkling as to where. I think it safe to say the transplanting of 1951, has completely taken roots. Though I am a strong Kentucky Wildcats fan I am also an Ohio State Buckeyes fan equally or more. I was hoping the two schools would play for the NCAA basketball title this year so I would have no disappointment in whichever won. It never came about. Kentucky won so I and most other Hillbillies are happy.

Some Hillbillies I know were never satisfied here and eventually moved back to Eastern Kentucky. For me to do that now I could adjust if I lived long enough.

Mary and I considered a move to Missouri a few years ago. We put our house on the market and asked the good Lord if it was okay for us to move have the house to sell in ninety days for what we wanted in price. Ninety days and we look for a home near Troy and his family in Missouri. Ninety-one days and we remain where we are. We presently remain where we are. There are a lot of Hillbillies living in Missouri but this one can't move there.

Grandkids

Mary has had a cushion for years that states "If I knew grandchildren were so much fun I would have had them first". We all know the impossibility of that statement. it tells all how much joy and happiness grandchildren bring to the lives of their grandparents. They are such a blessing to us. We are made proud by knowing we have more descendants. Their accomplishments make us feel happy for their parents and make grandparents feel they did some things right while raising their own children. Grand children give grandparents bragging rights. We seem to feel more comfortable boasting of them than we were of our own kids. I always enjoyed going to my grandparents. The grandmothers went out of their way to do or fix some little thing extra. Granny Conley always had cupcakes or a cake baked. She loved to watch her grandkids and enjoy them. Granny Trusty always had huckleberries. She would give me a pint jar and a spoon. They were so good. Granddaddy Trusty almost always gave me something each time we went to visit. He kept me in pocket knives. He never paid a lot of attention to my sisters but always went out of his way for me. I don't know exactly how to define Grandpa Conley. I'll just say he was not kid oriented, seldom said anything to us kids, showed no enthusiasm in us being there. With Granny it was always her showing her affection for all her grandkids. After Grandpa Conley died Granny moved in with Aunt Ruthie, mom's youngest sister and still always showed her love for us.

Grandchildren today don't have the time for their grandparents like we did growing up and that sometimes brings a pain to our hearts. We still love and appreciate them. Mary had rotator cuff surgery last year and only one of ten grandchildren called her to check on her. I'm sure that was heartbreaking to her though she never mentioned it. I mentioned my disappointment to her. She replied that they were all busy with summer activities. There is so much more in activities to keep grandchildren occupied than when I was a child. Even then as much as I loved and appreciated my grandparents there were times I would rather be with my friends. We have accepted this fact as grandparents and our hearts still swell with pride with their individual successes of whatever type they are.

We never chose favorites from our ten grandchildren. We didn't with our own and tried to show each our love and thankfulness for them in being a part of our lives. I must admit that I personally have given more to our grandsons than to the granddaughters. I think I got this from Granddaddy Trusty because he seemed to know what boys wanted and needed. I have given both grandsons small caliber rifles and shotguns. One of the things boys do is hunt so I try to equip them for it. This does not mean I love Christian and Drew more than the girls I just want there to be a special bond between us like I had with my Granddad.

Why Did My Dad Die So Young?

This is something I have often wondered about since March 31, 1955. Six days previous to this date was Saturday March 26th. There had come a big snow the night before and Dad planned to attend Kosciusko Conference near Wabash, Indiana that day. He had driven Uncle Mitchell's 1951, Ford home the night before and left his 1949, Buick Roadmaster with Paul Griffith who was his assistant at the church in Lima. After starting the car he returned to the house for something and I remember snow falling on the brim of his hat before he came back in. He had refused to allow me to go with them and I wasn't happy about that. He left to pick up Mitchell and the next time I saw him was in a casket. I was told Mitchell was driving as they entered a curve and the car spun around and was hit by an approaching pickup truck. Later that morning Paul came to our house to get Mom. We had no phone and he informed us of the wreck. Dad was in a hospital in Lima. The following Thursday evening she came home from the hospital and I asked about Dad. We were at her parents and she gathered all four of kids around her to tell us the news. An experience I have relived for over fifty-seven years in my mind. After I was grown I thought how difficult it must have been for Mom to tell us the news, the agony she had to feel all the way from the hospital knowing what she had to do. Paul Griffith did the funeral, Joe M. Wireman sang one of Dad's favorite songs "Egypt Land", Chad Burkhart prayed, but something else, something unusual for a funeral service which stayed in some hearts. Dad's mother, Granny Trusty shouted and praised God. Dad's youngest brother Troy came on emergency leave from the Marine Corps and told me a quarter century later that he did not understand Granny being able to shout in such circumstances. He said he understood it now though. Granny was praising God because even with the pain in her heart of losing a son, she was thankful that God was merciful enough to her that he took the only son she had who was prepared to meet Him. Brother Chad Burkhart told me later that Mom had asked him to pray in the service. After getting to know Chad later in life I certainly understand why Mom wanted him to pray. When he prays it is as though he is personally in the Lord's presence with honor and reverence speaking to Him. One man told Chad he would drive fifty miles just to hear him pray. So would I. The funeral was over Dad was buried and I was shocked that none of the family stayed afterward. As a boy of ten I didn't understand this. I remember the funeral procession from the church to the cemetery was well over a mile long. I was told there were enough people had to stand outside the church after it was full to fill it again. Dad was well respected, recognized as a man of God and was dead one month and eighteen days before his thirty-seventh birthday leaving behind a thirty-two year old widow to raise four small children. For this I have never been bitter and though I often wondered why I have never asked God why. Not even before I accepted Christ.

The church in Lima which Dad had served as pastor had many problems over the next few years. I have thought if Dad had lived would it still have had those troubles. From that church and some of the people won to Jesus there three other churches have spawned in this area. Churches that still see people saved today. Rom 8:28 says "And we know that all things work together for good to them that love God, to them who are the called according to his purpose." This was difficult to understand for years after Dad's passing. After accepting Christ I concluded that God always knows what He is doing and He has everything under control. Still without an answer to the question that titles this section my mind thinks of what might have been. But much greater than those thoughts are what lies ahead for all God's children. One day I will meet Dad, though he won't be Dad to me then, and we can praise our Heavenly Father together. That is one thing I would have loved to do in this life but didn't get to. I'm sure the wait will be worth it.

Little People Have Big Ears

It has amazed me what kids come up with from time to time. There were times when growing up I knew the grown-ups were discussing things I was not to hear. By straining I could sometimes catch bits and pieces but never mentioned them to the adults whom I overheard. Ten year olds and above have a good understanding of most things they hear or think they hear. The younger the child things they hear are not completely understood. I came to realize that I was unaware of what little kids think about things they hear. The imagination I have of their thought processes fascinate still me after all these years. When Alvin was a few months shy of the ripe old age of three he stunned me with what he said. I have from time to time over the last forty-four years broke into a laugh remembering that particular incident. Cledies Holbrook was visiting at our house one evening after work. We were in the kitchen Mary, Cledies, myself and a little fellow with BIG ears, Alvin. Cledies looked out the kitchen window and noticed someone moving into the house across the street. He asked who was moving in there and Mary told the woman's name. Her first name was Pat and I won't give the last name for the sake of her family. At that particular time in her life she had a reputation to be promiscuous. Years later she came to Jesus and lived for him the remainder of her life as a dedicated follower. When Mary told her name Cledies said "She's probably going to set her up a cat house." Nothing else was said. I had not even noticed Alvin being in the kitchen. A couple days later I drove up town for something and Alvin rode along. Returning home turning the corner to park at our house the now occupied house was directly in front of us as we made the turn. Alvin says "Over there's that cat house". My chin probably dropped to my chest. The first reaction was where did you get that and it hit me that I knew where he obtained that definition was from the remark by Cledies. My next thought was to tell him the solution that popped into my head. I said "That is not a cat house and I don't want to hear you ever say that again. That's Pat's house." He nodded consent so I got out of the station wagon and walked around where he was sliding out of the seat on the passenger side. I hear him saying softly "That ain't no cat house. They ain't no cats lives over there." Immediately my mind began to picture what had most likely what went through his mind when he had heard what Cledies said days earlier. I imagined he pictured a house with many more than just a few cats living in it. he probably thought since cats were small there were probably dozens in each room. The lesson learned was know who is listening *before* you say something. Look around before speaking. I would never have thought Alvin would have conceived in his mind what I have pictured his thoughts to be these many years. This incident with Alvin reminds me of the one about the little girl in Sunday School class and the teacher asks them "Where does God live?" This girl knew where he lived so she raises her hand to get the teachers attention. The teacher calls for her to tell the rest of the class and she was so proud to know the answer. With pride she says "He lives in our bath room." Her teacher isn't expecting this answer so she asks the girl why she said what she did. The girls answer was "Every morning my Dad pounds on the bath room door and yells 'My God, Are you still in there?' " A child's perception is sometimes incredible to say the least. Notice them when they are giving thought to something they are told or overhear. Then ask them their thoughts and consider yourself to be blessed.

Parental Control

I am not referring to television and internet use which technology has made available the last few years. What happened to parents controlling their children? This absence has damaged much of American culture. The term "playing both ends against the middle" has been around as long as I can recall. It simply means to try to make two people or groups compete with each other in order to get an advantage for yourself. Kids have learned to do this in some cases almost to perfection. While we were raising our boys often one would ask either Mary or I for something, usually not an item but an activity approval. If they asked me and I said ask Mary they went to her. If she said "Ask your Dad" they replied that they had and he said to ask you she realized the decision was hers. If the procedure was in the opposite order and I was told they asked Mom and she said ask you both Mary and I knew it was "Harry Truman time". The buck stops here and the decision was made singly or we talked together and gave an answer. Some kids learn that their parents don't use or even know what "Harry Truman time" is. They ask one parent and if the answer is "no" they immediately go to the other parent trying to get the opposite answer. Certainly they never inform the second parent that the other has already denied that request. When parents disagree in front of their children the child observes and takes mental notes. They decide quickly how to use what they hear to their advantage.

Our boys came along near the end of the Dr. Spock teachings. I read some of his methods on child rearing when Mary and I were expecting our first. My classification of the Doctor was not as a dignified practitioner. I had absolutely zero experience in raising a child. However I did have a vivid memory of my childhood. I knew Dad and Mom expected certain behavior with particular boundaries and if I exceeded those limits there was a penalty to be paid. After doing what I knew I was not permitted to do I was not told "Now that's a no no". We never had a wood shed but I received the same treatment available in the shed. One Saturday night at Church I sat with Roger and Danny Wireman, Joe M.'s sons. we were in the back of the church sitting behind two men whom I did not know. Danny had some paper which he tore into small pieces about the size of an adult's thumbnail. The one man had his hair combed as they did in the early 1950s, with it swept back over his top scalp. Danny took those small papers and placed them on this man's head. He had enough hair on top of his head that he couldn't feel it. All I did was snicker almost silently a couple times. I had no idea Dad saw anything. Young rule breakers are careful not to be seen. After church we got in the car to go home and Dad turns to me and gives me the bad news. I'm going to get whipped when we get home. If I can fall asleep and be asleep when we get home surely Dad won't wake me just for a whipping. No way can I go to sleep. We pull up in front of the house. Slowly I get out of the car and walk to the gallows. I know it wasn't a death sentence but Dad whipped hard. He didn't whip us often but we all knew that when he finished the point would definitely be made clear. We had a weeping willow tree in the neighbor's yard that had lots of branches hanging in our yard. Dad went through the front door on through the house and out the back door. He returns with a handful of willow switches with the leaves jerked off. He took me to the bedroom had me lay my trousers aside then turned me every which way but loose. I squalled, screamed, hollered, danced, and did everything except talk in tongues. believe me I was good in church for a while to come. I feel I should point out here that Dad played no favorites. I don't know what the girls did in church that night because I wasn't near them so the rod was not spared on them that particular Saturday night either. Dad was fair with us kids. We knew the rules and the penalty for breaking them. I feel the Bible has told us God has informed us of the rules, of what He expects of us, and the penalty for disobedience. Dad told me something I did not believe before whipping me, "This is going to hurt me more than it does you". Years later Mom told me when Dad would have to whip one of us that later he would get off to himself and cry. He didn't enjoy disciplining us but knew it had to be done and was his duty. So looking back I believe it did hurt him more than it did me. Today parents have spared the rod and spoiled the child. Sometimes the rod is needed and sometimes other means can accomplish to need. The summer of 1954, a neighbor across the street, Ron and I decide we are going to smoke. We pitched in some change and bought a pack of cigarettes which we buried in our garden. We dug where the corn was tall enough we could squat or sit and not be noticeable. We agreed that each time we smoked we would put some money in the coffee can we used so when those smokes were gone we would have enough to replenish them. My sister just under me, Pixie, caught us and we gave her a cigarette knowing this way she doesn't dare tell on us because she has been smoking too. As a young girl I don't think she ever kept a secret. Ron and I got her to promise she would tell no one. When Dad got out of the car after work she met him and spilled her guts. "David's been smoking." I knew I was in trouble. That night before bed time dad says "Son, I want to talk to you". Here it comes a lecture and then a whipping. I was shocked by Dad's first words when he told me he wasn't going to whip me. He simply asked me to give him my word that I would not smoke until I was old enough. I was nine then and am now sixty-seven and have never gotten old enough to smoke. I think Dad realized that by the time I was old enough to smoke I would be smart enough to know better. I deeply cherish that thought.

I always told our boys that if ever I see them put a cigarette in their mouth I would bust them with my fist even if I was so old and feeble I had to crawl to get to them. They all probably puffed at least one but neither of them smoke.

I remember hearing Bob Harrington, The Chaplin of Bourbon Street, say "Smoking may not send you to hell; but, it will make you smell like you've already been there". That statement comes to mind almost every time I am near a person who reeks of tobacco smoke. It gets in your clothing, hair, beard, and anything it touches.

"Fair Fight Trusty"

All my youth I had Dad's side of the family tell that my Great Granddad had killed a bear with his fist. I believed it because they had no reason to lie. During the first few years I preached travelling different places sometime I would sing with my sister Karen and others. At different churches people would come up to me after finding out my last name was Trusty and ask if I was related to "Fair Fight Trusty". I never heard of him. They then asked who my family was. I always told them the same thing, Alvin was my Dad, David C. was my Granddad, and his dad was Rube Trusty. I spoke at Denham, Indiana Free Will Baptist church one Sunday morning and an elder Brother named Dudley Trusty came up after service to ask if I was related to "Fair Fight". When telling him the same genealogy I always told he said "You're related. It was Rube". He invited me to come to his home that afternoon and he would tell me some things. He knew Rube and his brother Newt. Their names were actually Reuben and Newton. One day Newt an Rube and another man were out and ran upon a bear. Since Rube had always bragged he could kill a bear with his fist he was told to prove it. He went up to the bear and clobbered it. The bear got mad and did what came natural by attacking Rube. Dudley said the bear was ripping Rube to pieces and he asked Newt and the other man "Boys, if you don't help me this bear's gonna kill me." Their reply was "Nope, it's a fair fight this time Trusty". Rube was able to get in a lucky punch and killed the bear or Newt and the other fellow would have stood there and watched the bear kill him. After this story was told people began to call Rube "Fair Fight Trusty".

You may have heard or read the statement "I shook my family tree and a bunch of nuts fell out". I am both amazed and shocked by what would fall out of my family tree. When Bo's son Drew was a junior in high school his daughter Lynsey was a freshmen. Both played Varsity basketball. That season the games scheduled conflicted a few times because the boys and girls teams were both scheduled to play on the same nights. The Athletic Director does the scheduling. I sent an email to Bo to forward on to the AD, coach Baker. Bo wouldn't forward it on. Later I told coach baker about it. The email started by asking not to make scheduling conflicts the next season because it forced not only grandparents but parents as well to choose which child they would watch that night. I continued by saying "Let me tell you a little about my family. I told him everything written above about Rube killing the bear with his fist. The rest was similar to this. My Granddad, after whom I am named carried a pistol all the time. The only time I knew that he allowed a man to continue breathing after telling him to set down and shut up was in church. My mother was at the church they called Baptist Bottom between Lackey and Garrett, KY. Mom told me it was winter time and Granddad had been over to Quicksand to see Rube who was gravely ill and on the way back home they came upon the road being blocked in front of the church. Granddad came inside to get cars moved so they could get by. Mom said the door opens and you could hear the wind howl, she turned around and saw Granddad enter. He walked down the center aisle telling the preacher who had just rose for his sermon "You fellers got the road blocked. Get them cars moves so we can get through. The preacher tells Granddad "We are having church. Get over there and set down and shut up." Mom said she knew she was looking at one dead preacher because nobody spoke to Dave Trusty that way because he would shoot them. Granddad turned white as a sheet turned around twice saying, "I said you've got the road blocked and get them cars moved and I mean now". Mom told me there were men jumping over seats to get to the door. She decided to catch a ride back to Lackey with Granddad and followed him to the car. She said there was only one car there. The one Granddad was riding in.

My Dad when growing up loved to fight. Dad's brother Troy told me about this part of his life. Troy said Dad would pick a fight with anyone he could. At no time did any three ever whip him. Troy said on occasion four could do it but most of the time it took at least five. I said to Uncle Troy when he told me this "My Dad?" Dad was only five feet six inches tall weighing one hundred thirty-five pounds. Then I told coach baker "I'm tougher than all three of my predecessors put together. Keep that in mind when you make up next year's schedule.

I then wrote from Psalm 23, "Yea thou I walk through the valley of the shadow of death I will fear no evil" and added "because I am the meanest toughest dude to ever set foot in that valley". He knew I was only joking about my toughness and would never do anything except make a choice whether I would watch Drew or Lynsey play if there was a conflict in the schedule. Coach Baker had a good laugh and all the next season he would come up to me and ask if I had killed any bears that day. I love to laugh, joke, and have good clean fun. God intended for life to be enjoyable for His greatest creation.

Using humor by injecting it at the proper moment in a sermon causes people to remember the message but more importantly it helps get across the point, and is easily and comfortably received by most listeners.

Granddaddy was a poor example of a parent when Dad and his brothers and sisters were growing up. He did everything a married man and parent shouldn't. He was a scoundrel no doubt. He never accepted Christ until the year after Dad died, 1956. Afterward he told something that shocked me. Though Granny was saved she carried a pistol for protection under what we always called "granny dresses". They were loose fitting and I never noticed any bulge. He never owned a car so every time they went some place they either walked or had someone to drive them. Granddad said there were about three years of his life when he was afraid to walk in front of Granny because he had treated her so badly he was afraid she might shoot him in the back. Some of the things I have been told he did I figure if Granny had not been a Christian she quite possibly would have shot him.

Dad was in the Army during WWII, with the job of providing security for the Manhattan Project at Oak Ridge, Tennessee. There was another Kentucky native stationed with him who was a Christian. Some of the other men teased Esbon Taylor because he was serving Christ as a young man. Dad overheard an incident and stepped in to defend Esbon. Dad said he would whip anyone who bothered Esbon. They had a friendship that lasted all Dad's life. Dad wasn't saved at the time he was in the Army, but held in esteem those who were and lived the example they should. Mom and Esbon's wife became friends after Dad died writing letters and Mom went to their home once for a visit.

In the 1980s, Dad's brother Troy attended a revival at a Church of God in Wabash, Indiana. Troy was good friends with the pastor who introduced him to the preacher who came from Tennessee to preach the services. When told Troy's last name was Trusty the preacher said his dad had been in the Army with a Trusty from Floyd County, Kentucky, named Alvin Trusty. This travelling preacher was Esbon Taylor's son. Isn't it amazing the things God does? The odds of something like this happening I think would be astronomical. It never ceases to amaze me when I consider some of the things God does such as Troy meeting Esbon's son.

When Will I Die?

Being mortal means we have the liability of death hanging over us. Death came upon mankind because of what transpired in the garden of Eden. Genesis Chapter three tells of the conversation which took place between Eve and the serpent (the Devil). He enticed Eve and she yielded to the temptation then got Adam to partake also. The penalty had been told them well in advance of their fall. So death came to all humans of the world. therefore all of us will face death unless Jesus returns prior to that experience. Death is feared by the living. Scripture calls it the king of terrors. I have known some people who were so afraid of dying they would not go to church because preachers talk about death and how we must prepare to meet him. Job 14:5 "Seeing his days are determined, the number of his months are with thee, thou hast appointed his bounds that he cannot pass;" Here God has told us the number of days we will live has already been determined. None of us can extend that time. A familiar quote is "When your number is up, it's up." Paul also said that not everyone would die in his letter to the Church at Thessalonica. We shall not all sleep but we shall all be changed. All will die except those Christ catches away at his second coming. All those caught up to meet him in the air and those resurrected will change from natural bodies to spiritual bodies. More than thirty years ago I heard Billy Graham in one of his televised Crusades make this statement. "I look for Jesus to return today. If He doesn't come today tonight when I go to bed I'll look for Him to come before morning. If He doesn't come tonight I will look for Him to come tomorrow. If He doesn't come tomorrow I will expect Him tomorrow night." All Christians should look for Him every day of our lives with anticipation. Over the years I have developed a mental picture of one day God leaning over to Jesus on His right hand and saying "That is enough, Son. Go get My Church." Whether I die or not is placed entirely in God's hands. If I face that day I anticipate being like most people and having a certain amount of fear. But yet I'm sure I will face it with some expectation. I expect to go to sleep and awake at the trump of God and the voice of the arch angel as I burst from beneath the sod and rising in the air springing forth to meet my elder brother, Jesus to forever be with Him. For those not saved and having no personal relationship with Jesus it is easy for me to see that for them to face death would be pure agony. I feel there is some uncertainty in death, some things about it we don't understand, some uneasiness perhaps as a bride and groom on their wedding day. Realizing there are some unknown things about the step they are taking they are somewhat scared. Will we get along as well as we have during courtship. Each thinks of compatibility? If the engagement has been short they may think what is the other one really like? One thought that never entered my mind was Is Mary as beautiful on the inside as she is on the outside? I found out that she is and Thank God for her. Death has been chasing me since December 19, 1944. If or when it catches me I want to be like Paul and truly say I have fought a good fight and kept the faith. Therefore there is reserved for me a crown. A reward of life eternal in the presence of God the Father, God the Son and God the Holy Spirit. I will be a winner for all eternity.

Recently after a funeral service I officiated while walking past the funeral coach to the funeral director's car I told a good friend working for the funeral home "I hope Jesus comes back before I have to ride in there".

The reward awaits at the end of the journey and what a great trip it has been and continues to get better all the time.

Great Friends

I have been blessed to know, be friends with, and worship with some memorable people. I will talk about church people first so I will begin with preachers. My favorite of all preachers I have known is Rev. David Rowe. We became acquainted in 1967. He was also on the Ordination Council when I was ordained into the ministry. Some preachers you hear leave nothing seemingly worth recalling. With my memory declining in the last few years I can still remember almost every message I heard David deliver. The first time I heard him was in October 1967, at Kosciusko Conference when convening at the Erie Street Church in Wabash, Indiana. The Pulpit Committee selected him to preach the morning session. David speaks distinctly and is easily understood by all listening. His first few words caused me to think that we had an educated speechmaker that morning. He chose as his sermon 1 Kings 20:23, "And the servants of the king of Syria said unto him, Their gods are gods of the hills; therefore they were stronger than we; but let us fight against them in the plain, and surely we shall be stronger than they." Using the thought that God is not only God of the hills but also God of the valleys. Before he completed that sermon I knew I had never heard better preaching. When I was ordained he brought forth from Pilate's words about the sign above Jesus cross titled "What is written is written." As we became better acquainted over the years I could see why he was such a powerful preacher. He lived his daily life practicing all he preached and taught. David had an older brother named Aaron with whom I became good friends. A very dedicated Christian. I am so thankful and feel so privileged to have spent time with these two men of God. Aaron was called home in the 1980s. David is in his eighty's, has macular degeneration and other physical problems but still has the same dedication he has always had. I talk to him now and then on the phone and the last time we spoke I told him he was still my favorite preacher. He humbly and graciously thanked me for those words.

I have heard some great preachers in my life without having had a personal relationship. The opportunity of that type of relationship never presented itself. To name just a few I must mention the late Dr. B. R. Lakin, Dr. Melvin Worthington, Rev. Dale Burden, Rev. Ronald B. Cannon, and Rev. Hurtis Stone from Mansfield, Ohio. These men accomplished some enormous things for the Lord. Those that I have personally spent time with and feel I must mention will have to be shortened or I could go on for many pages.

Joe M. Wireman was very influential in my life. In my youth I thought no one could beat him preaching. Rev. Roy Burkhart was an active pastor until around age eighty-two. Roy was called home just recently at age ninety. He was getting Alzheimer's and entered a nursing home about a week before going to be with Jesus. The night before he died he walked the halls preaching God's Word well into the night. That tells me where his heart really was centered.

Rev. Chad Burkhart, younger brother to Roy is quite a person. Chad is humble, loves the lord, and gives his all for Jesus. He and Roy each had much influence over the lives of hundreds of people leading them to Christ and assisting them in the course of their Christian lives. One of the churches Chad served had the opportunity to purchase additional land across the road. Chad wanted them to buy it and when some of their leaders discussed it one spoke up and told them that if they bought it they wouldn't own it fifteen minutes before "that preacher will want to build something on it".

Rev. Clarence Tolliver is someone I have as much respect for as any Christian I have known. He has always been faithful, caring, humble with a remarkable singing voice. He has always been supportive of anything that would benefit God's church.

Rev. Eugene Webb touched the lives of so many people during the years he served the Lord. He always wanted to talk about the Lord, cared so much about people and their souls, and gave of himself sacrificially for the Glory of God. His wife, Carolyn (I jokingly call her Sister Hardshell) was with him every step of his ministry. They sacrificed a few years of their lives to be house parents at our children's home near Greeneville, Tennessee.

Dr. Alton Loveless came to Ohio and proved to be a great blessing to Free Will Baptists here. Having a great business ability and leadership quality his years spent here moved our denomination forward in many ways. Leaving Ohio he was replaced by Rev. Edwin Hayes as Ohio Free Will Baptist State Promotional Secretary. Edwin and his wife Linda are on the road almost every weekend with him speaking in one of our churches. He goes wherever invited. We always enjoy him preaching for us where I pastor. He runs our state office with excellent business management skills and still finds time for numerous revivals each year as well as attending the various Conferences we have in Ohio.

Dr. Freddy Dutton has so much to be said about him it is difficult to know where to begin. God has blessed Freddy with an ability to touch people's hearts like no one I know. His sermons always seem to leave the congregation wanting more. He has an ability to inject humor at just the proper place and time. His desire to win souls to the Lord is so obvious. His wife Terry has had bouts with serious illnesses and still travels with Freddy most every time he goes. Freddy also has tremendous skills in woodworking. He is studious and never satisfied to rest on past accomplishments always wanting to tell someone else about their need for Jesus.

Joe M. Wireman, Lesle Wireman, and Joe's son Eddie have touched countless lives. With Joe and Lesle having been called home Eddie remains faithful though his health isn't good. Another Wireman preacher showing great potential is Brandon. His youth, enthusiasm, study habits lets me know that God continues to call young men who are willing to make the personal sacrifices and have the commitment in their hearts to give their all for His will.

I'm sure there are countless men whom God has called and are doing His work that I have neither heard speak nor met. God bless and keep them all.

During all the years I travelled I had opportunity to be in Sunday School classes in different churches. Three men who taught classes stand out in my mind for their ability to expound God's Word. One is my uncle Troy, the others Gerald Dials and Bobby Howard. The lasting impression I have comes from their knowledge of the Bible and the personal experience of preparing to teach a lesson properly. The time it takes for preparing is enormous. Most people go to their Sunday School class having only quickly read the printed lesson and feeling comfortable about their effort. Preparing to teach a class takes as much time and effort as preparing to present a sermon from God's Word.

Since childhood I've enjoyed fishing on occasion. You must have bait to catch fish. Jesus told us to follow Him and He would make us fishers of men. Fishing for fish I can stop and buy the bait. Fishing for men I've found I have to dig for it. That digging is made possible by what God has presented us to use for the bait. The Bible.

Recently I saw Jim Stimmel, a former classmate who lives in Wyoming and has been used of God to start four different churches there. When we said good-by I made him the promise that "If we never see each other again I'll meet you on the other side in heaven."

Mistakes

Ask yourself one question. Am I perfect? Being honest we must admit none of us are. I once asked a friend I had not seen for some time "How are you?". His answer was only two words, "Pretty good". Since we always joked a lot I told him the Bible said there was none good (Mark 10:18 And Jesus said unto him, Why callest thou me good? there is none good but one, that is, God. KJV) only one and that was God. I also told him we both knew he wasn't the least bit pretty so his answer wasn't true. I said "You just won't tell the truth, will you?" He caught the joke and we shared a laugh which some would have thought corny. Since scripture tells us no one is good the logical conclusion is that we all do make mistakes. We do some things we should not and fail to do some things we should. These two things describe two types of sin, commission and omission. With the sin of commission I exceed the boundary of what is acceptable to God. Draw a circle and place one dot inside it. The inner part of the circle is what God accepts. The dot is you. You are confined to the inside of the circle to remain within God's will. Outside the circle represents what God does not want us to be and where He don't want us to go. With the sin of commission I leave the circle to go where God does not want me. The sin of omission is represented by another circle the inside of which God is happy I am there but He wants me to go outside the circle to witness to those on the outside to try to get them to come to Christ. Since I feel comfortable within this circle I decide not to leave it's comfort to do God's bidding. The lines of each circle, and two circles are required to fully understand what I am saying, are limits. One I must remain within to please Him and the other I must step outside to please Him. We each as Christians have either or both went over the line or fell short of the line at some point in our walk with Jesus. Mistakes vary therefore we should always be aware of the lines and where they are at all times. The best way to keep track of the lines is found in this scripture. "John 5:39, Search the scriptures; for in them ye think ye have eternal life: and they are they which testify of me." (KJV) The more we know of the Bible the less temptation we will give in to. The more knowledge of God's Word we accumulate in our mind and heart the more we will be able to come to the aid of those who need help. The easier it will be to point folks to Jesus. It will help us to not exceed or fall short of the proper line. Basically the Word of God, the Bible, has within its pages all answers we'll need in this life. We just have to search them out.

Why I Am Faithful To My Denomination

I grew up in the Free Will Baptist, was saved in Free Will Baptist, baptized by Free Will Baptist. Did that make me a Free Will Baptist? The answer is "absolutely not". I joined them of my own choosing. My best pal through high school was Emmett. His family was Pentecostal even though he did not come to Christ until after we had been out of school a couple years. Most Pentecostals I knew then felt that Baptists were "okay as far as they went. They just didn't go far enough". There were nice folks at the Methodist churches, other Baptist denominations, the Missionary church, and others. Where did God want me to settle? There is a story of a Baptist pastor talking to an elderly lady about coming to his church. She informed him she was born a Methodist, raised a Methodist, and that made her a Methodist. He asked her "What if your parents had been idiots what would that have made you?" Her answer was "A Baptist I guess". So I studied the Bible, researched doctrines of various denominations and after no small or minor effort decided I would be Free Will Baptist. It was not because it was the denomination of Dad and Mom. It was because all the digging I did brought me to the conclusion that their doctrines and teachings paralleled the Bible as closely as any I studied. That was a lot of years ago and I still hold the same conclusion today with an even stronger grasp. We have some of the best and brightest in our denomination. Such men as Dr. Thigpen, Dr. Alton Loveless, Dr. Robert Picrilli, L. C. Johnson, and the list could go on and on. One of my favorites is the late Rev. Bob Shockey, so down to earth with a depth of dedication I admired greatly. Free Will Baptists have a global vision of promoting Christ for the salvation of all the world. All Christians should have that same vision. The late comedian Dave Gardner in one of his comedy routines said of Cuba after the Cuban missile crisis was past "The Mississippi National Guard riding on a flat bed wagon could take Cuba in fifteen minutes". This quote may not be exact but is to the best of my recollection. Free Will Baptist has the best doctrine in the world. That, along with enthusiastic dedicated people within the denomination has been responsible for the saving of thousands of souls. We teach the correct recipe to bring people to Christ. We are saved by grace through faith. It is not by works but the gift of God. Christ became lower than the angels so that His sacrificial payment for our sins and then His resurrection from the dead promises us that after our resurrection we will then be equal to the angels. I am proud of our denomination and plan to remain faithfully involved in it. However Free Will Baptists have not cornered the market on Christianity nor are we the only denomination that is truly Christian. All denominations and even non-denominational churches and independent churches have problems that arise. Some situations are easily handled while others we face advice and assistance can help with the solution. The structure of the Free Will Baptist organization offers what can be needed. We have the local church which is its own governing body, The District Conference with whom the local churches voluntarily unite, then The State Associations comprised by the Conferences, and then The National Association of Free Will Baptist. All of the levels working together assisting one another is invaluable. Another great asset of our denomination is Randall House Publishing. They print our Sunday School literature which is not only used by Free Will Baptists but by more than thirty different denominations.

Why Do Really Good Friends Drift Apart?

When growing up I felt some of my closest friends and I would always remain attached as we were then. Our drifting apart was not done by making the decision to do so. Things happen in your adult life as well. We made no conscience decision to make this happen. It comes about primarily because our lives for whatever reasons take us in different directions. My best friend all through school, Emmett Manns, and I had great times growing up. He was far more outgoing than I was in our youth. After graduation he went to California and returned about thirty-four hours before I left for military service. We always got together when I took leave and came home. He married and was expecting his first child before Mary and I were married. He and Linda had two sons while Mary and I had three. We lived within a mile of one another but only got to see each other occasionally most likely because of work schedules and family obligations as well as church happenings. I never thought any less of him and probably not getting to see each other very much caused me to cherish the memories of the times we had growing up.

During the nearly forty years I worked making footballs for Wilson Sporting Goods I met and made lots of friends. The one with whom I was most comfortable and enjoyed his company most Was Charlie Moore. He was like myself, a Hillbilly transplant. His wife, Wanda went to the same school as I but was a couple years younger. She had one sister in my class. Wanda lost a battle with cancer but made peace with God in her heart and was well prepared when He called. I have managed to get Charlie to attend church only one time. It was before Wanda passed away. He said he enjoyed it and still gives me the same reaction he always has when I ask him to come. He always gives me a real big grin. We are both retired now and I miss seeing him on a regular basis. Charlie and Wanda were excellent parents raising their own children and two of Wanda's older sister who passed away unexpectedly. Our boys spent time with their boys and enjoy good memories. Our Church hosted our District Conference years ago and Pastor John Castle from Rittman, Ohio preached the message that session. He told of an experience he had going visiting and inviting folks to come to church. The following Monday morning at work the first thing I did was tell Charlie about it. Pastor John said he was going through a neighborhood in Rittman to invite people and one home he went to the man thanked him for the invitation but said he would be unable to come because he didn't have any peanut butter. John asked the man why not having peanut butter would prevent him from coming to church. The man replied "Nothing, that's just the first thing that came to mind". Charlie got a big kick out of this. You can already guess what excuse Charlie gave the next few times I invited him to church. "I can't Dave, I don't have any peanut butter." After this one Saturday afternoon Mary and I were at Sam's Club in Lima. Seeing the peanut butter I thought of Charlie so I bought a five pound can which I delivered to Charlie before we went home. I told him when he ran out I would get him some more. He never used the no peanut butter excuse any more. I pray for Charlie and want him to be saved. If people could go to heaven because of morality alone I feel Charlie would make it. But morality alone will not satisfy the Lord. We are saved by grace through our faith in what Jesus did at Calvary.

We also had church family during the time we were raising the boys. Truman Rowe and his wife Vernia were especially close friends. They had two boys close to Alvin and Bo in age so they played together a lot. We would often in warm weather get together for cookouts and other activities. Their only daughter Manoka is as close to a daughter Mary and I ever had. They are just a special family to us. As our children grew up went off to college and work which meant a residence change I began to notice a drifting apart. Not in our hearts because we never lost the love and respect we always had; but, in both our families we spent our free time getting together with our kids. God called Truman home several months ago and it has been one of the most heart breaking losses I have faced. He was such a dedicated Christian always actively doing something for the church. I am so thankful that the church honored him several years ago for what he meant to us all. I presented him with a plaque and the ladies gave a carry in dinner for all to come and show their appreciation for him. There was even a cake with the words "The best deacon in the state of Ohio". The appreciation our church shared is nothing compared to the one Heaven provides.

Shall I Re-Enlist?

In the Air Force I was assigned to Homestead Air Force Base and the 31st Tactical Fighter Wing, a part of the Ninth Air Force. Homestead was a SAC base which is explained ahead. The 31st was made of several Fighter Squadrons. Our Wing had F-100 Supersabre Fighters. Though I was a part of TAC (Tactical Air Command). For two and a half years I was attached to SAC (Strategic Air Command), which was a part of Eighth Air Force. TAC had the fighters and SAC had the bombers and tankers. I still remember the thoughts I had when viewing a B-52, Stratofortress the first time. It amazed me that anything that humongous could fly. In either January or February of 1965, my duties and attachment to SAC ended though not leaving Homestead. About this time I was asked by the 31st Wing Information Officer if I would like to come work for him. I asked about what the job would entail and jumped at the opportunity. I worked for Captain Joseph G. Martin about nine or ten months. He was very nice and quite easy to get along with. He was from Big Stone Gap, Virginia I recall and looking back I feel he probably reflected his upbringing the way he treated everyone with respect and dignity regardless of their rank or lack thereof. After several months the Captain got orders transferring him to Nellis AFB, NV. I hated to see him go as I considered him a friend as well as my superior officer. The Information Officer of an outfit is the right hand man of the Commanding Officer. He is a liaison for the Commander and the public media. Captain Martin went to Colonel Franklin Nichols, the Commander to get another job for me before shipping out. The Colonel had me assigned to an open job as a clerk in the Orderly Room of the Organizational Maintenance Squadron. I remained there until leaving active duty the following July.

The Information Office was in the Headquarters Building. Our office was next door to the Wing's Retention Officer which was staffed by an NCO (Non-Commissioned Officer), Technical Sergeant Duggan. His assigned duties were to try to talk men into reenlisting after their initial obligation expired. Sgt. Duggan would call people to his office for a "retention interview" which consists of reminding the person of the benefits of staying in the service for twenty or more years. The Air Force began these interviews after a year in the service. They continued near your enlistment anniversary each year. In your fourth year they call you in with eight or nine months remaining, again at about six months, then four, and then every time you turn around. More in a moment. In June 1965, half of the 31st was sent to Viet Nam. They stayed until December and then the other half went to replace them; but, they were to stay a year. I did not have a year remaining on my enlistment so I never had to go. In late march or early April 1966, our new Commander, James J. Jabara, who was at that time America's leading living jet ace, was at Ninth Air Force headquarters and was informed that somewhere around Thanksgiving every person in the 31st would be going to Viet Nam and only the Almighty knew how long they were to remain there. Within a few days Sgt. Duggan called for me to come for, guess what, a retention interview. I had already decided I wasn't going to be a career military man. They had missed their chance to keep me six months before when they declined to send me to Ft. Slocum, New York, to Defense Information School. I do not want to be coming to see Sgt. Duggan every other week and then more often as I got real short. The interview began with Sgt. Duggan going through his spiel about all the benefits etc. After a few minutes I stopped him saying "You think I'm crazy don't you Sarge." Here's how the conversation after my first statement. Sarge: "No, you're a sharp troop Trusty. You would be a great twenty year man." Me: "Tell the truth now Sarge, you really think I'm nuts." Sarge: "You would make a great career man. You have a family started, you're smart, the military would be great for you and your family." Me: "Sarge, I know you think I'm crazy. Let me tell you something. My mother only raised three idiots and they were all girls." Sarge: "You've got a good start already. Sixteen more years and you can retire, set for life." Me: "Look on my sleeve Sarge.

If you knew the midnight oil I had to burn just to keep those stripes. Not get them. Keep them." Sarge: "Now you know Trusty that you've got it made here." He tries to get me with the benefits talk. Me: "Sarge, last week Colonel Horne called us all to the hanger on the flight line and told us everyone is going to Viet Nam in a few months. With my luck I'll get killed over there". Sarge: "You'll be alright. You can handle yourself okay." Me: "Sarge, you're wasting your time with me. They won't let me re-up." (re-enlist) Sarge: "Why not" with a surprised look. Me: "Because I've got back trouble." He has all my records in front of him and picks up the medical folder and looks through it. Sarge: "There's nothing here about you having back trouble. What's wrong with it?" While holding my hands in front of my chest and the fingers all pointing toward the ceiling and hands about a foot apart I answered. "I've got a yellow streak about a foot wide that runs right up the middle of it." Sergeant Duggan who was a distinguished looking man lost it. He jumped up throwing his arm in front of him pointing to the door said, "GET OUT". He never called me again to come to his office. I knew what to say to get the reaction I wanted. I didn't want to be bothered with his interviews. Not because of him he was a professional soldier and did his job well. My mind was already made up. In July I plan to go back north.

Inviting people to church and trying to persuade them to commit their lives to Jesus doesn't work the way it did with Sgt. Duggan. I knew the magic words to get the reaction from him I wanted. I haven't found those words to persuade people for Jesus. People are different and therefore react differently. However, I will always continue to try reaching them for the Saviour.

Don't Make Her Nervous

In the spring of 1975, I was asked by Pastor Melvin Staggs to come preach revival services at South Side Free Will Baptist Church in Wabash, Indiana. We had a good revival and I met some folks I had not previously been acquainted with and have appreciated the relationships that came about because of that invitation. I distinctly remember an elderly gentleman called Mr. Coffman. He was 89, years old without looking it, seemed very spry, and was a treat to talk with. He complemented me on the sermons of the revival saying he enjoyed hearing me. On Friday night he told me that he wouldn't be there Saturday night due to other plans. He returned Sunday. He knew he needed the Lord in his life but never made a single move toward allowing Him into his heart. Years later I spoke to Melvin about Mr. Coffman and learned he had died. Before dying he asked his daughter to call Melvin to come see him. She refused telling him he didn't need to talk to that Hillbilly Preacher. She had not been raised in church, and so was unaware of the need for salvation for her dad or herself. It broke my heart to hear this since Mr. Coffman was keenly interested in his soul but not enough to do something at the time he was invited by the Holy Spirit. The night the revival closed I drove back home.

At that time we were living in an older house in the country. There were some outdoor cats there when we moved in and the boys played some with them. Some were more tame than others. One was without my knowledge expecting. Mary and the boys had not been with me in Wabash that night and when I arrived home she told me of the exciting births. Bo, like me always had a tender spot for about any animal and so was worried about the delivering mother. Troy was like a bull in a china shop. Only four at the time he was unaware of the delicateness of the situation. One of the boys noticed this mother cat under the kitchen floor having kittens. Troy wanted a good look and wasn't careful about getting it. Bo was worried about the mother cat and watched the blessed event happen. Mary said Bo was trying to keep Troy from interfering and told him, "Don't make her nervous and she will have a whole bunch of them". Days later Bo was describing the births to some of his friends as they sat together in the back seat of our car going somewhere with us. Bo said, " I tried to keep Troy quiet so she would have a lot of kittens. She had the first one as I watched her. Then she lifted her leg and another walked out." Hearing that analysis made it hard for me to concentrate on driving. I don't remember how many times that mother cat lifted her leg or how many "walked out". One thing certain I will always remember the way Bo told it.

Some people seem to have no compassion for animals. I have always loved cats and dogs. It bothers me to see a dog or cat have to be outside in cold weather or be mistreated by anyone. One of Dad's friends, Earl, told of when he was a boy he had a dog that his father would not allow him to bring in the house. He was saddened by that fact. I know from experience there is no relationship like the one between a young boy and his own dog. They can really have an attachment to one another. Earl said one day his dad told him to go fetch his dog and he would housebreak him. Earl was all excited because now he can bring his dog inside which will be great for both he and his dog. Earl calls his dog and it comes. He brings the dog to his dad to be housebroken. His dad takes a ball peen hammer and thumps the dog on the top of its head. The dog is addled and as soon as he has some stability takes off running as hard as he can. Earl's heart is broken, his dad was to make the dog able to come inside the house, not kill it. Earl's dad looked at him and told him his dog was now housebroken. "He won't ever come close to this house again." How cruel this was.

Some Things Kids Say

The 1950s had some great television shows. Art Linkletter had a show I really enjoyed where he had children he would talk to. Some of the things they said were so funny he wrote a book titled "Kids say the darnedest things. It was full of humor as only children can perceive things to be. I mentioned elsewhere of Troy using the words "scrunched and un scrunched". Bo had a good one that makes me wonder and imagine what actually he did think at the time. He wasn't yet four years of age and we had been to the North Judson, Indiana area for me to speak at a church in that area. Some of Mary's family lived there also. We were at her brother Cecil's home and the kids were playing when the ladies finished preparing something to eat. Since it was warm weather all ate outside with the kids sitting with one another. Later as we returned home Bo asks Mary a simple question that even all these years later sends my imagination soaring. "Mom, do people have tails?" She told him that in a sense we did but not like animals. Mary wanted to know why he asked. Bo told her that when he sat down on a huge rock to eat his cousin Randy came over to sit beside him. Randy said to him "Move your tail" to give him room to sit no doubt. I still imagine Bo probably turning around and looking behind himself to see if he had a tail. He probably thought since he had never seen his tail and never felt it that it probably comes out on its own without us knowing it is out and visible by others.

When Troy was in scouts they were planning an overnight camping trip. They were to meet at the front of the school at a certain time. We only lived a block away so he packed his gear and walked over to the school. After arriving he thought of something he was going to take with him and forgotten to pack it. He comes back home to get whatever it was and returned again to the rendezvous site. They had already left. I glance out the living room window and saw him coming down the alley back home again. I stepped out on the porch to ask what he had forgotten now, when he exploded in tears saying "They ran off and left me". My emotions kicked in seeing how broken hearted he was. You can do me wrong and I can let it slide or completely ignore it. But not when it comes to my baby. My mouth spoke the very first words I thought letting them out as I thought them. This should never happen I know and I am ashamed of myself for it. "That makes me so mad I could whip every one of them". As soon as the words came out I wished they hadn't. My mouth was put into motion without my brain being in gear. I think to have him put all his stuff in the car and we will try to catch them. If we can't I can drive him to the camp. About that time here comes the scouts pulling up in front of the house. Someone has reminded them that Troy wasn't among them. As the cars came to a stop Troy is no longer broken hearted. He is mad.

The words that screamed from his mouth were, "My Dad is so mad he could whip every one of you". I am embarrassed to say the least. The scout leader glances at me with a sheepish grin. He too is embarrassed they had erred in leaving without making sure all going were loaded. Think before we act or speak. Sometimes we fail and it causes some situations most of which will at least bring a blush of embarrassment to our faces. Occasionally it brings much worse.

Scripture teaches us that a wise man will keep it in until afterward and a fool utters all his mind. Often we speak without thinking. I find this so especially with young inexperienced folks.

Stand Here Bo

For several years we lived in an older house that had some things many newer ones did not. There was no furnace and duct work to distribute the heat properly to each room. This wasn't a problem as Mary and I had each grown up without those items. Dad and Mom's house has an upstairs as did the one we were currently living in. Those two houses each had a ventilator that permitted the warm air to pass through the ceiling of the first floor and through the floor of the upstairs. In winter the air rising through a ventilator was warm and made the upper story warmer. The house Mary and I lived in had the ventilator situated just a little forward of the heating stove. One Sunday afternoon Alvin and Bo were playing upstairs while Mary and I sat on the couch in the living room. Troy had not yet been born. She and I were talking when Bo came falling through the ventilator to the floor in front of us. It happened in a flash, swish and he passed through. He was not hurt in any way but it scared him badly. Alvin had removed the metal part on the upstairs floor and told Bo to step down and stand on the bottom part. Being unaware of any danger he did what he was asked to do. Fortunately he fell through straight down. Had he not it could have been disastrous. Alvin it seemed could always persuade Bo to do what he himself would not. When Troy was big enough for Alvin to try it on him he wasn't very trusting of Alvin. That was probably because Alvin picked on him.

Are We There Yet?

When the boys were young we visited Mary's dad often. The trip was in excess of three hundred miles if we travelled Interstate 75, and some less than that if we took US Route 23. If we went for the weekend we normally left home on Friday after working hours. Invariably we would get into heavy traffic on these trips. Usually the boys would be in the back of the station wagon playing. A few times we would be less than twenty miles from our start when one of the boys would ask "Are we there yet". When driving in heavy traffic when all lanes are moving at or in excess of the speed limit you don't want to hear that question. Naturally Alvin was the first to ask that question. Within fifteen minutes Bo would ask and that would be followed by Troy. So trip after trip it was the same old thing. Alvin did give us a slight variation though. One time instead of asking the dreaded question he said "Dad, Are we having traffic"? We had never heard that one before. And yes, we were having traffic.

My Favorite Sport

In high school I loved basketball at every level. we had a good high school team with lots of talent. At the same time I was in high school Ohio State basketball was at the top of their game with Jerry Lucas, John Havlicek, Larry Seigfried, and other players who put the Buckeyes at the top of college ball for three years. Winning the national championship game in 1960, with the best players only sophomores they were expected to take all the marbles the next two years. The 1961, and 1962, seasons had them playing for the top prize each year also but Cincinnati Bearcats beat them both years. The championship games were good games with close scores with the Bearcats proving to be just a little better than the Buckeyes. During this time I enjoyed watching Bill Russell of the Celtics and Wilt Chamberlain of the Philadelphia Warriors play against one another. I remember when Wilt scored one hundred points in a game and it was great to be a Wilt fan. I liked Bill Russell because he was so good defensively. Over the years I enjoyed college ball always admiring great coaches like Fred Taylor of the Buckeyes, Dean Smith of North Carolina, Al McGuire and his Warriors from Marquette. My admiration for John Wooden of UCLA still continues to grow even now after his death as I learn more about his life.

Football was a sport our high school didn't have so I knew little about it. The first football game I ever attended was in the Orange Bowl. It wasn't the Orange Bowl Game however. The Miami Hurricanes played all their home games there so I went with some of the GIs in my outfit. The only time I knew where the ball was during the game was if they threw a long pass. George Mira played for Miami at that time and was always mentioned in the local papers in Miami. The stadium was shaped like a horseshoe and our seats were in what Bob Uecker would call "nose bleed heaven" in the curve of the shoe and most of the game was played on the other end of the field. I felt that experience was wasted money on my part. After leaving the military I usually watched one football game a year, Ohio State and Michigan. My admiration for Woody Hayes began from him being a great humanitarian. As I learned more about the game of football Woody and Bo Schembechler inspired me to learn more about it. Now, though I had the privilege of seeing Yogi Berra, Roger Maris, Don Larson, and the great Mickey Mantle play baseball I still prefer a matchup between Bo and Woody, two greats at the college level. For the NFL my favorite team has been the Steelers. I root for other teams and players also, some for their playing talent and some for the class they present to the world. Tom Landry and Don Shula were great coaches I admired along with Chuck Noll and Joe Gibbs. John Elway, my favorite quarterback ever, "Mean" Joe Greene and Jack Lambert, Ronnie Lott, Roger Staubach, and of course Earl "the Pearl" Campbell all were fun to watch. Those I enjoyed most were at the high school level some of whom went on to play in college and some didn't. I love them best because they played initially for the love of the sport. Naturally I enjoyed watching our boys play but there were other high school players that impressed me more.

Alvin and Bo had a sense of where the ball was but Chuck Moore, Charles and Wanda's son, was the best defensive player I ever saw. He made plays that had I not witnessed personally it would be difficult to believe if someone told me of them. Offensively Ben Mauk was the best I ever seen. Though Bo was defensive coordinator where he coached and I loved watching his team I missed numerous of his games to go watch Ben. I don't really know how to describe his play as it was unreal. Several games I saw he basically "put on a clinic". One playoff game in Tiffin against Margaretta I remember describing to our son Troy over the phone. I told him Ben engineered two long time consuming drives, each was sixty-some yards. One was six seconds and the other was seven seconds. What makes high school football my favorite sport is the enjoyment the players have and their enthusiasm when a play is successful. They play only because they love the game itself. There's no money, no free tuition, just the fun the game brings. Of course there is always the sense of accomplishment.

The game also teaches great lessons that equip the players for life's ups and downs.

Making Dad Real Proud

One of Bo's classmates accepted a scholarship to play basketball at Rio Grande in Southern Ohio. Jimmy Kearns was the single best basketball player I ever saw in high school. He was the Division IV player of the year in 1985. I remember a game in which he scored sixty points. Personally I think he could have averaged between forty and fifty points per game. He was a team player all around. Sometimes I think he passed off when he actually had a better shot than the person getting the pass. All games I watched him play I don't recall a single play that he deserved criticism. He was really that good. Academically he was intelligent, just a son any parent would be proud to have. His younger brother Jason was a very good player also. He hit two free throws in the clutch to win a state championship; but, Jimmy was better.

While he was playing for Rio Grande his team was scheduled in Tiffin, Ohio. With it being only sixty miles away I wanted to go see him play. I think Bo had already made plans to go with someone else when mentioned it to him that I was going to go. Jim Matthieu from our town and I had made plans to go together. I picked Jim up and we drove to Tiffin. During the trip he told me something he witnessed Bo doing. Jim had a daughter with whom Bo was friends. Once Bo was visiting Lisa and she introduced him to a friend of hers from another town. This girl asked Bo to go out with her. Jim, overhearing the conversation told me he could hardly believe what Bo told the young lady. He told her he couldn't because he was going with another girl at the time and when he was going with someone else he never cheated on them. Jim told me he was amazed because most college boys Bo's age would have never done that. Jim said that he felt what Bo did was a direct reflection of how he was raised. Just writing this I may have to go purchase a larger shirt because of my chest swelling.

Tombstones

Years before I heard Dr. David Jeremiah say anything about epitaphs being one of his interests I ran across something on the internet that made me curious of the same thing. I have dozens which I copied from the internet. Still on occasion I spend time searching for others I haven't copied. Some of the things inscribed on headstones make me wonder why relatives have such printed on them while others cause me to see what I think was the intent. Some have titles of songs, pictures of favorite activities, such a large variety today. When Dad died the norm was name, date of birth, date of death. The stone Mom chose for Dad and herself had those dates and she also had Dad's picture in the center of the stone. At the bottom she had scripted "Founder of Lima Free Will Baptist Church". I always looked on it as a last honorable tribute by her to Dad's life.

Here are some that bring a smile to my face.

In Stowe, Vermont, "I was somebody, Who is none of your business."

In a cemetery in Georgia B. P. Roberts name appears under the words "I told you I was sick".

In Winslow, Maine,
In Memory of Beza Wood Departed this life Nov. 2, 1837 Aged 45 yrs. Here lies one Wood Enclosed in wood. One Wood within another. The outer wood is very good. We cannot praise the other.

My favorite is: Under the sod and under the trees lies the body of Jonathon Pease, He is not there it is only the pod: Pease shelled out and went to God.

In a Ribbesford, England, cemetery: The children of Israel

wanted bread and God sent them manna, Old clerk *Wallace wanted a wife, and the devil sent him Anna.*

In a Thurmont, Maryland cemetery. Here lies an Athiest All dressed up And nowhere to go.

One I cannot recall the name or place was what a husband placed on his wife's stone.

"Here lies my wife of 47 years and this is the first thing she ever did to please me."

What do I want on my tombstone? Honestly, I have never given it any thought. I will let Mary decide. In the not too distant future we would like to purchase our grave sites and order a stone. Whatever she wants will satisfy me. Hey, when I'm there I will be asleep waiting for Jesus return. When that happens **Stand Back** because nothing will interfere with me meeting Him in the air.

What's Next?

Often we think in terms of a single goal in life and when we reach it the satisfaction is only temporary or was less than expected. We want a new car which takes a good length of time to make having one come to fruition. After a couple months the enthusiasm which was so strong weeks before has disappeared. After the new carpet is installed and the first item spilled on it we lose the thrill of how nice it looks. The first stain on it we start picturing and planning the type and color we will replace it with.

Ask what's next after life ends. Giving it serious thought can we answer it with absolute truth knowing there is no chance we have deluded ourselves? If Jesus returned in an hour or death knocks on our door in an hour can we know beyond any shadow of doubt that we are prepared for either event?

To answer that question we need to look at what the Apostle Paul had to say about it.

Second Timothy, Chapter four, verses one through eight will give each of us the answer to the question. Addressing verse two: Not everyone is a preacher but all are ambassadors. Always be ready to tell people about the Lord. Tell people what the Bible says and leave no doubts in their mind that you believe and stand on the Word of God. If they teach something wrong call them on it. Try your best to inspire others to consider and accept Jesus. Do it patiently, not of anger but allowing them to see the love of Christ in you. Verses three and four: This reminds me of the time we are currently living in today. They have so little knowledge of the Scripture it will be up to us as Christians to lead and guide them toward the truth. Verse five: Living Christ centered lives, enduring whatever may come our way, whether it be criticism, mockery, harassment, etc. Making full proof of our ministry tells us to live the same consistent Christian life each day allowing people to take notice. We don't have to point out to people each thing we do to tell them it is because we are His servants. I have found that their observing our lives speaks far more than all we could say.

Always trying to win some lost soul to Christ using whatever talents the Creator has given us. Trying to live each day of our lives making efforts to live so people can see Christ in us. Verses six through eight: Facing the nearness and inevitability that death is coming or Christ is returning we know in the deepest part of our heart without even the most minute portion of doubt that we have lived each portion of our life in a manner that assures us God is satisfied with it. And there is no fear of facing the Judge of all mankind. There is expectation in our hearts and an anticipation in our hearts far greater than a small child has the night before Christmas.

Through the years I have been present more times than I can remember during the last moments of people's lives. Also I have researched the dying moments of many, some famous, some unknown, some Christian, and some who desired no part of Jesus.

I was alone with my mother's oldest sister when she passed. It was so sad because she wanted nothing to do with God and had told my mother so.

The great preacher Henry Ward Beecher brother of Harriet Beecher Stowe said "Now comes the mystery" just before dying. Certainly there is some mystery in death but I am confident that when my eyes close for the last time it will be a temporary thing. Christ shall awaken me in His likeness. The Psalmist said "I shall be satisfied, when I awake, with thy likeness".

Following are a few last words I copied long ago:

Cardinal Borgia: "I have provided in the course of my life for everything except death, and now, alas, I am to die unprepared."

Napoleon: "I marvel that where the ambitious dreams of myself and of Alexander and of Caesar should have vanished into thin air, a Judean peasant—Jesus—should be able to stretch his hands across the centuries, and control the destinies of men and nations."

D. L. Moody: "I see earth receding; heaven is opening. God is calling me."

William Shakespeare: "I commend my soul into the hands of God my Creator, hoping and assuredly believing, through the only merits of Jesus Christ my Savior, to be made partaker of life everlasting; and my body to the earth, whereof it was made."

Martin Luther: "Into Thy hands I commend my spirit! Thou hast redeemed me, O God of truth."

John Milton (British poet): "Death is the great key that opens the palace of Eternity."

Charles Dickens: "I commit my soul to the mercy of God, through our Lord and Savior Jesus Christ, and I exhort my dear children humbly to try and guide themselves by the teaching of the New Testament."

Andrew Jackson: "My dear children, do not grieve for me . . . I am my God's. I belong to Him. I go but a short time before you, and ...I hope and trust to meet you all in heaven."

Joan Crawford said to her maid who had begun to pray aloud for the actress, "Dammit...Don't you dare ask God to help me".

James French, a convicted murderer, was sentenced to the electric chair. He shouted these words to members of the press who were to witness his execution. Hey, fellas! How about this for a headline for tomorrow's paper? 'French Fries'!

Frightening is the thought of closing your eyes for the last time on earth and immediately being surrounded by the flames of hell. Everyone should wish to leave with words like those listed above who knew in their hearts they were going to a better place.

Beetle Bailey

My favorite comic strip is about the goldbricking soldier and those who serve at Camp Swampy. The CO, Commanding Officer, General Halftrack has heard nothing from the Pentagon in fifty years and still has only one star. Sergeant Snorkel is continually on Private Bailey like ugly on an ape. Miss Buxley, Killer, and some real misfits comprise the rest of the outfit. Lieutenant Fuzz reminds me of the typical second Louie. A ninety day wonder, an educated idiot are some of the terms we used when I was in the military. Mort Walker certainly put together a winner to become my favorite comic strip. There are others I like but this one is the best for me.

We had a second lieutenant we nicknamed Donald Duck. The military police before each shift holds guardmount. Guardmount is the time fifteen minutes prior to going on duty that the duty sergeant and or duty officer has the opportunity to inspect the troops and tells everyone their assignment for the upcoming shift. This information was always posted at the end of the last shift we had completed the day before but was repeated in case there had been some changes made. Another item for guardmount was any new information coming down the chain of command or any new policies going into effect. One day at guardmount Lt. Donald Duck informed us of the following: "It has been brought to our attention that some of you are blousing your boots at the first or third eyelets when regulations specifically call for all boots to be bloused at the second eyelet". BIG DEAL!!!

Two or three weeks later I pick up the comics from Sundays paper and turn to my favorite. They are in the headquarters building in a staff meeting when gen. Halftrack asks if there is any other item before the meeting is adjourned. Lt. Fuzz speaks up "It has been brought to our attention that some of our men are blousing their boots at the first or third eyelets when regulations specifically call for all boots to be bloused at the second eyelet". I'm confident someone in our outfit had written Mort Walker about what our Lt. Donald Duck had recently passed on to us. I don't think it could have been just a coincidence.

After getting married and living off base one afternoon I had been somewhere in a patrol truck and returning to the control room as they were getting ready for the upcoming shift change I walked down the hall toward the control room and Lt. Donald Duck was standing near the end of the hall deep in thought having one arm across his stomach with the other arm's elbow resting on it and rubbing his chin. He sees me and asks what I'm now doing. I told him I just finished with what I was doing. This was standard, you either just finished or were almost finished. In south Florida in summer the dust would cling to our boot soles and there were dusty boot prints going down the hall to the control room. The educated idiot said to me "Get a piece of felt cloth and put it on the end of a stick and wipe up the footprints as they go in and out." Being the good troop I was I said "Yes, Sir", went out to the parking lot got in my car and went home. Where am I going to get some felt cloth? Second lieutenants were the dumbest creatures I met in my four years of active duty.

One exception was Lt. Dunlap. One night someone was shooting near the edge of the base. We did not know what they were shooting at but couldn't take the chance they were shooting at our B-52 tail sections.

Someone decided they were in a small wooded area and patrols were dispatched to search. Lt. Dunlap never told anyone of the nine of us "You go in here, you go there, etc". He looked at us and asked "How many of you guys will follow me in there?" After that I felt I would wade through fire to take him a drink of water. He earned our respect and it is so much easier to follow a respected leader. Another reason being a Christian is not difficult for His sacrifice and the love it took for Him to make it earned our respect.

And Then There Was Schwartz

In 1964, a fellow came into our outfit who looked as normal as anyone, was friendly but not outgoing. He was assigned to another duty section so I only saw him momentarily as we changed shifts and then not each change time. He would wave, smile, nod, or say "Hi". We never really got acquainted. One night we had an alert readiness exercise. When that happens they put the recall into effect and everyone reports to their duty station. After reporting we were all just milling around waiting to see how long it would last or if there would be any specific happenings. During the milling around I saw Schwartz standing with a group and nobody was talking to him. I walked over and asked "How's it going Schwartz?" He said something in answer to me that I have no idea what it was. I asked what and something came out which was nothing legible. I thought to myself "How did this guy ever get into the military? He can't even talk. I have just met the first blooming idiot that's not a second Louie. I thought they had the market cornered."

Not all things are as they appear is something I had been taught all my life. Turns out Schwartz was far more intelligent than anyone had credited him to be. He had a friend in the Miami area he spent off duty time with who had a little red Volkswagen. One day his friend calls police to report his car stolen. Metro Dade County spots the car pulls it over and arrests the driver. With the driver being an active military man immediately the base is notified. This took place on a Saturday afternoon when military personnel activities are not on duty. The commanding officer is notified that one of his men was just arrested for grand theft auto. Homestead is a SAC base (Strategic Air Command) and at that time SAC used what they called the MCS, short for Management Control System. The way MCS worked was your outfit is awarded points for good things and points are deducted for bad things. Some commanders seemed to ·spend too much effort and focus on MCS as far as most of the soldiers felt. Our CO calls some officer in Personnel and has the paperwork taken care of to discharge Schwartz within a couple hours. Naturally Mr. Schwartz's friend had to take care of some personal things and the police are unable to contact him for a few hours. Finally returning home he calls to see if there is any word on his Bug. He is informed they have it and the guy who stole it is locked up. He goes to pick up his car and asks who the low life is that stole it. They say some Air Force guy named Schwartz. He says Schwartz's first name and is told he is correct. Now he says that Schwartz didn't steal the car, they are good friends, close enough he had even given Schwartz a key. "He just never told me was going to use it. I can't press charges against my best friend."

Mr. Schwartz is released from custody and no longer in the military. Smart move. He had everyone fooled. I thought him to be a near lunatic. I summarized him by what I saw on the outside in only one weird conversation. The Bible says that man only looks on the outward appearance but, God looks on the heart. God knows what is in each person's heart and mind which gives Him an insight we will never have. I learned from this to not size up a person from a single incident. We need to know more, much more.

In the 1970s, I became acquainted with another Schwartz, actually two brothers. Bernie and Raymond. Both are good hearted people. I have been around Raymond enough I realize that he is a lot like a wart. He does grow on you. Ray has a personality that people are attracted to. He loves Jesus, likes to have fun, enjoys fellowship, and is very active for Christ. He is gifted mechanically and electronically and amazes me with some of his talents. He lost his wife, Jean some time ago and continues to be the same ole Raymond. He is always helping people and sets a great example of what a Christian truly is.

Going North

In our youth we make dumb decisions and do silly things. I had twenty-nine days left in the military and took a fifteen day leave. We came to Ohio and visited my family then went to Indiana to visit some of Mary's family. Then I returned to Homestead for the final two weeks of my enlistment. during this time I made the rounds to try to see friends in the military police barracks and others in headquarters squadron.

In the MP barracks a casual friend from Indianapolis named Duncan (last name) found out I was going to LaPorte, Indiana and he was starting leave the same day I was getting out asked to catch a ride with me. He said we could switch off driving and drive straight through and he would share the cost of gasoline. I told him it sounded like a winner to me and the agreement was made.

I was released from active duty Friday July 29, 1966, at one o'clock in the afternoon and heading north we stopped at the gas station where I had worked part time filled up the tank and said good-by to Snuffy. I made a short stop in Deland which was an extra eighty miles to say good-by to cousins living there. Then it was on the Florida turnpike which ran into I-75. We went west enough somewhere to get on I-65, which took us into Indianapolis. Saturday morning before noon Duncan was asleep in the back seat as we cruised up I-65. I was holding it steady on one hundred and five miles per hour just floating along when I noticed a black dot in the rear view mirror. Back then I had heard of a fairly new radar system some police were using called "Vascar". They were supposed to be able to clock your speed about two miles away. I thought of this new radar as the black dot kept growing as it gained on me. I figured he already had me clocked so I may as well eat up all the road I could before I was pulled over. As it turned out it wasn't the police but a fellow in a brand new 1966, Plymouth Sport Fury. I'm still at a hundred five as he swishes around me as though I'm parked on the side of the highway. My guess was he was doing at least one hundred forty miles per hour.

I continue on north and after a few miles the Sport Fury is sitting in the median with the man inside appearing to do nothing. A few miles later I see a black dot growing in my rear view mirror again. I'm thinking it's either a cop or that nut again. It was the nut, again swish like I'm sitting still. A few miles north he again is in the median. This happened five or six times. What I thought at the time shocks me today when I think of it. In the sixties a Chrysler Corporation auto had a tendency to heat up when the engine was ran hard. I figured he ran it for all it was worth while keeping an eye on the temperature gauge and when it got over so far he would stop and allow the engine to cool. I don't know this is what he was doing only I guessed it was so. I'm thinking "You dummy. If you would slow down and drive a reasonable speed like me it wouldn't heat up". Like a hundred and five is a reasonable speed.

Today this memory makes me think of how people are and the way we look at things. We are always right the way we do things, it's always the other person who is wrong. Because this man was speeding an additional forty miles per hour over my speed made him no dumber than I. I was doing thirty-five miles per hour over the posted limit and he probably had the limit doubled. We were both stupid and our actions were inexcusable. When we are young we give no thought to how near our actions and deeds bring us to tragedy. I no longer drive like I did in my youth. After retiring I purchased another truck and sold the one I had driven to Bo he jokingly told Mary one time I ruined that truck because he would look down at times and be doing only forty-five. I think he had noticed my speed when riding with me locally.

There is a poem I recall from my youth that says "Sing While You Drive".

At 45, sing "Highways Are Happy Ways"

At 55, sing "I'm Just A Stranger Here, Heaven Is My Home"

At 65, sing "Nearer My God To Thee"

At 75, sing "When The Roll Is Called Up Yonder I'll Be There"

At 85, sing "Lord I'm Coming Home"

Some People Are So Heavenly Minded They Are Of No Earthly Benefit

I have heard this said throughout my adult life and usually referring to particular individuals. One lady who wasn't a Christian asked me if I knew a certain brother in the church. I said I did and he was one of the most dedicated men I was acquainted with. She told me she would much rather talk with me than him. This surprised me because she had only known me for a couple years yet had known the other man since childhood and they both were near the age of my parents. When I asked her why she felt that way her answer was "He only wants to talk about God and the church, at least you will talk about other things." I replied that was probably because of his dedication to the Lord.

Jesus said in John Chapter16, that His followers are not of the world. So Christians are in the world but not of the world. Dr. Melvin Worthington defined this better than anyone I ever heard or read. Dr. Worthington was at the time he spoke at the Ohio State Convention of Free Will Baptists in the 1980s, the Executive Secretary of our National Association of Free Will Baptists. He stated that Christians are "in the world living distinctly different from the world as a testimony to the world".

Since Christians are in the world I feel we should make the best of our time here. Let us enjoy life to the fullest having fun. One of the things that hindered me from accepting Christ sooner in my life was the impression I had that once you became a Christian everything about life had to be totally serious, that the days of fun were over. Using a word which Gomer Pyle always said "Goooooollly" was I ever mistaken about my view of being a Christian. I accepted Jesus the fall of my Junior year in high school and discovered how wrong I had been. I actually had more fun the last two years in high school than I ever thought possible. I attended school social activities conducting myself differently than before and the enjoyment just got better all the time. I was in our class plays both Junior and Senior years which was fantastic.

Share The Blessings
That Come Your Way

Each year at Alger High the senior class had an unofficial "Senior skip day". It was unofficial because it was not authorized by the school and was actually planned secretly by those who were going to participate. Not every Senior took part. The day before our planned day one of my classmates, Jim Smelser, and I messed it up. We left the music room after class finished. I had study hall the next period and stopped in the hallway before entering the study hall. I made the comment about what the music teacher had said about the next day saying we didn't have to care about it because "we're not going to be here tomorrow any way". After being in study hall a few minutes I was informed that I was wanted in the Superintendent's office. I went there and when I walked in there was Jim whom I was with in music class and in the hall way. When I saw him I jokingly said "Whatever it is I didn't do it". He added that he hadn't either. The Superintendent calls us into his office and closes the door beginning the conversation with, "Between classes I was standing in the hall way and overheard.....". He said he heard one of us say we wouldn't be at school the next day and was curious as to why. I told him I intended to work for Arthur Push who was building a new home which was true. I don't remember what Jim said but even at that age I was able to recognize a song and dance when I heard it.

The Superintendent informed us that he had been at other schools where things like this had happened and they did not end well. He said the students involved got to go through graduation and got their diplomas like every other graduate but the diploma wasn't worth anything because they were unsigned. Instantly I decided to come to school the next day. In the lecture we received the point was clearly made. I thought of not naming Jim for the following reason. The Superintendent at the end of his lecture asked if there was anything else planned that he should know about. There wasn't but my friend Jim evidently wanted to share what we had received from the boss man so he said "I think the Junior class was planning the same thing for tomorrow". We were told to leave and go back to our scheduled classes. When we were in the hall again I said that I had no idea the Juniors were planning a skip day too. The reply was "They're not". All this was in the morning. Our first class after lunch was in the Junior class home room and when we arrived we had to wait a lengthy time before we could go in. They were getting the same verbal thoughts we had gotten earlier that day. And they had no idea what it was about. However there were two people in school that day that knew why. Most of the Junior class had a blank look on their faces when they exited the room. I still get a good chuckle when remembering this.

I fully believe God wants us to have fun as we live as long as we stay within certain boundaries. If we relate to some people on something other than religion there is always the possibility of it leading later on to getting around to their need for Christ.

The Apostle Paul told us that he had become all things to all men that by all means he might save some (lead them to Jesus). Let us strive to be what God wants us to be, do His will, and always reach out to others because we want them to have in their hearts and lives what we as Christians have.

Humor is something almost everyone will respond to.

It's Not Just A Job It's An Adventure

The U. S. navy used this as a recruiting slogan at one time. How would this apply to being a Christian?

One of the strongest motivators for me in accepting Christ was fear. I had heard preaching about the fire and brimstone of hell since I was a small boy. I had read a significant portion of the Bible and believed without a doubt God would punish in eternity all who refused to accept Him. There were other motivating things but fear was the strongest. I did not want to risk being lost forever and ever. As my relationship with Christ grew the fear of disappointing Him was and is remaining. The big surprise for me is that it isn't nearly as strong as it was when I got saved. 1 John 4:18-19, states "There is no fear in love; but perfect love casteth out fear: because fear hath torment. He that feareth is not made perfect in love. We love him, because he first loved us." A personal relationship with the Lord is based on love. The law which Moses received had no love. Therefore it was weak and could not give life, but when Jesus came demonstrating the love of God the law of Moses was fulfilled. I serve God from a deep love in my heart which I am sure would never have been there had not He loved me first. As our love increases the fear wanes but never disappears. Simply, the Bible teaches that "The fear of the Lord is the beginning of wisdom".

In the military I did as told because of the repercussions that would await if I failed to carry out each directive. It was my job to do as told. With Jesus it isn't a job or at least it doesn't seem or feel like one because I do it enthusiastically.

From 2 Kings 10:15-16, "And when he was departed thence, he lighted on Jehonadab the son of Rechab coming to meet him: and he saluted him, and said to him, Is thine heart right, as my heart is with thy heart? And

Jehonadab answered, It is. If it be, give me thine hand. And he gave him his hand; and he took him up to him into the chariot. And he said, Come with me, and see my zeal for the Lord. So they made him ride in his chariot.". Years ago I preached a sermon that I titled "Come ride with me in my chariot".

Certainly you can believe me when I say my life as a Christian has been a tremendous adventure. Words fail me to be able to adequately express what a ride it has been. There have been high times which to me are mountain top experiences. There have been times facing some situations that I felt almost alone and then remember Jesus had said He would never leave nor forsake us. Every Christian faces them and with patiently waiting and trusting in God, each thing we face, He works out for His betterment.

My uncle Troy after whom we named our youngest told me an experience he had. He lives in Wabash, Indiana where there are plenty of churches. One Sunday evening he attended service at a local Church of God. Before the service began a young man came in that he had never seen before. Troy said the Lord placed in on his heart to give this young fellow five dollars. Troy said I thought "I can't Lord, all I have until I get paid is ten dollars to get back and forth to work and eat on at work. He said the feeling kept getting stronger all through the service. At the ending of the service Troy said he shook hands with the young man and slipped a five dollar bill into his hand. He said he made out fine until payday came and happy he was obedient to the Holy Spirit. He attended this same church for Bible study each week even though his membership was with another church. Many months later their organization was having a week in Jellico, Tennessee, and that pastor invited him to attend. Thinking it over he decided he would go so he arranged for a week of vacation time from work.

When he arrived to register he found out he was assigned to a room for the week with someone0 else. He walked into the room and a young man was lying on one of the two beds. The man arose and Troy told him he looked familiar. He told Troy he was the young man months before who stopped in at the Church of God in Wabash and Troy had slipped him a five dollar bill. He then explained what that small amount of money did for him by getting him to his home in Warsaw and back and forth to his job. He told of having been somewhere and the return trip when he got to Wabash he was out of money completely and knew he never had enough gas to get him home. It was as if the lord had led him to that church. He gave Troy a huge hug thanking him for what he had done. Troy confessed to him "I didn't want to give you the money but it was like the Lord kept insisting upon it". Troy said the Lord blessed them that week to have a most joyous week, hear great preaching, have good Bible studies, and enjoy everything that went on during that week. Just another part of the adventure that God doesn't restrict to just a certain few. He does things for all His children.

In the winter of 1963, one morning at Homestead Air Force Base I went into the mail room in our barracks and in my mail was a letter from home. It was as if the Holy Spirit said to me "Karen got saved". I opened the letter and that was the news from home. They were having revival and my oldest sister had come to Jesus. Just so many things He does to assure us that we still belong to Him and His love is always there.

For approximately ten months I travelled to northwestern Indiana every other weekend to help a church without a pastor. During this period I became acquainted with Gaston Combs. He wasn't saved yet but would not miss church at all. His wife Margaret was such a super lady who wanted so much for her husband to accept Christ. They would travel out of state on vacation or visiting relatives but Gaston insisted they must be back home for Sunday morning church services and Sunday School. During these months Gaston demonstrated a dedication for attendance that was stronger than many Christians. I think he felt an obligation to this particular church even before he came to Jesus.

Through all the Sundays I spoke Gaston was definitely interested but never made a move to come to Christ. This puzzled me and caused me to study more to try injecting new subjects from different angles. Still he did not respond. Months after I stopped assisting there at a New Year's Eve service Gaston came forward and received Christ as his personal Saviour. I was unaware of this until one evening of the following week I answered a phone call and heard Margaret greeting me. She asked what I was doing on a particular Sunday. The Holy Spirit spoke to me and my answer was, "Coming to North Judson to baptize Gaston." She had not told that was the purpose of the call. Gaston wanted me to take part in his baptism. What an honor for me. Gaston has remained as dedicated as any Christian I know. He is still back home for Sunday School and morning services at his church. The church later selected him to fill the office of Deacon and he does it well. A few years after this he and I were talking and he relayed to me what was surprising to me. He said, "I never forgot the first time I heard you preach. You preached a message "Come ride with me in my chariot. That has always stuck with me."

In 1971, Mary's grandmother from Paintsville, KY., passed and we attended the funeral. It was on a Saturday and we spent time with her dad before starting back home for Sunday services. Our station wagon had a headlight go out so I stopped at a gas station to have it replaced. There was a man standing inside the station who kept staring at me. Finally he spoke and said "You're a preacher aren't you?" I said I was. He said "I heard you preach in Indiana where my brother was going to church." I don't recall which church but he told me what I spoke about.

Sometimes I feel like the message is a failure and later someone tells me how much they enjoyed it. Some I feel I have done a good job and no one mentions anything about it. So I try to be like Avis and "Try harder".

When I remember Gaston's compliment I think of this scripture. From Psalms 126, verse 6, "He that goeth forth and weepeth, bearing precious seed, shall doubtless come again with rejoicing, bringing his sheaves with him."

In May 1970, I attended the Northern Ohio Free Will Baptist Conference which met in Bucyrus, Ohio. Their pulpit committee selected me to preach that afternoon. I knew very few people there. A few weeks later I passed a fellow I worked with who had his brother with him in the car. His brother said "That's the guy who preached about the Rooster's Sermon at our Conference. Bob told me the next day at work what his brother said when he saw me pass. The Lord is so good to all people how can we not show our appreciation?

That Big Bad Standifer Family

One of Mary's brothers had a disagreement with his wife many years ago and she made the above statement. Mary's family is a large one and a close one. They are as close as any family I have ever been around. They love one another and always express it in various ways. When they get together for any occasion you can feel the affection among them.

Some folks think that seven is a lucky number. Mary is number seven of her brothers and sisters who totaled eleven that lived. There was a girl long before her that died very young. I never met her mother as she had already passed on before we met but I conclude for Mary to be the person she became her mother had a great deal to do with it. Mary's dad, Zack Standifer, as a young man had his back broken in the coal mines. I was told they afterward carried him home and laid him in the bed. When his back healed he was bent forward approximately thirty degrees. Never able to work again he still managed to provide for a large family. They told about an instance when he purchased a huge truck full of bicycle parts, putting them together to make a lot of bikes and sold them. He was a proficient trader also. By this I was told he was so good at trading that he could take a pocket knife to town and when he returned home he might have maybe a milk cow, cash, and other things.

There were six boys in the family and five girls with none being lazy. All have good work ethics and habits. Most if not all the boys are like their dad in that they like to trade and are shrewd doing so.

The entire family worked to get ahead for the benefit of their families. All raised respectable children in a manner they can be proud of. All the family treat people respectfully.

Joyce, the sister under Mary has a heart as big as all outdoors but don't ever let her think someone is doing any of her family wrong. The youngest boy, Charles used to have an appetite I could hardly believe for as slim as he was. Joyce and Mary said he "ate so much it almost killed him to carry it". When Joyce and Charlie were in high school some boy said something to him that Joyce didn't like and she had that boy whipped before he knew what was happening.

I told Joyce and Mary that when they get together there isn't the equivalent of one complete brain between the two of them. They get so wrapped up in each others' company they lose all sense of reality.

There is nothing bad about the Standifer family. They are happy fun loving people with a great variety of talents from athletic abilities to craftsmanship to musical ability.

John told me of an event between two of his Dad's brothers Lindsey and Bud. I never met either to my knowledge. What John told me caused me to figure that trading things runs quite deep in the Standifer family. One of the uncles had a dog which came up missing. No one knew what happened to it. The other brother saw a dog built like the missing dog but the colors of its coat did not match the missing dog. He bought the dog for a small amount took it home and painted it so the coat looked like the brother's dog. He loads the dog in his truck then drives over to the brother's home. When the brother sees the dog he is sure it is his dog. His brother says "That isn't your dog. I just bought him and have a lot of money in him". Still convinced it is his dog this brother said "I know my dog when I see it. That's my dog". The reply is "No it isn't your dog". This conversation goes back and forth until the one who brought the dog over offers to sell the dog. Naturally he must make a profit of some sort since he has so much invested in the dog. The deal is made and the selling brother goes home with a big profit from the sale of the animal. In a few days it rains and the current dog owner realizes he has been suckered. But he knows his brother did not lie to him because he had insisted "he's not your dog".

Years ago at Ohio's State Convention of Free Will Baptist the young adult choir from Southwest FWB Church in Columbus sang at the Friday evening service. Their pastor, John Meade said they were available to visit other churches occasionally. They were remarkable so Truman Rowe asked them to come to our church for our next session of Conference to be hosted in McGuffey. They sang for us at McGuffey and all churches of the Conference truly were blessed by it. The church hosting each session of Conference always serves lunch and all can fellowship which is truly enjoyed. Pastor John was overheard by Mary to say he was originally from the Paintsville, KY., area. Her grandmother had lived there so she asked John if he knew any Standifers. He said, "Do I know any Standifers? I married one." His wife Carolyn sang with the choir and Mary told me she kept thinking she looked familiar but didn't know who she was. They were first cousins who had not seen one another in far too many years.

There is nothing bad about the Standifer family. I told John Meade I got the best one of them all. Understandably he feels he got the best one.

There is a lot of talent in the Standifer family.

Cecil had two sons, Randy and Sean, who could play about any musical instrument that had strings.

John had two sons and a grandson who were really athletic. Tony was a great basketball player recruited by big time colleges and decided not to play. Tim was awesome in football. Tony's son, Andy played football at Purdue as their long snapper. In the bowl game one year Andy had flags thrown against him for two separate violations on the same play. At least it got his name mentioned on national television.

All the girls are good cooks, parents and caring people.

I am so grateful that God allowed me to be a small part of this great family.

My prayer is that for all those Standifers who haven't yet accepted Christ will do so.

The Scissors

While working in the Information Office with Captain Martin we needed a pair of scissors. The process of obtaining them was unimaginable for a person who never had to get something the military way. I thought I could fill out the requisition forms and walk to supply and pick them up. That isn't how it's done. That would have been too easy. The proper procedures must be taken to get anything.

I fill out the requisition forms.

Place the forms in Distribution (daily mail for only on base) addressed to Procurement.

I wait for the scissors while Procurement does its job.

The forms probably arrive at Procurement a day or two after I put them in Distribution.

At Procurement the forms go to an in box on someone's desk to be checked over.

The forms may stay in that particular in box for either minutes, hours, days, weeks, or however long if that person would be on leave, lazy, or hasn't had their four hundredth cup of coffee that day. Nobody is in a hurry.

After the person whose in box the forms are placed gets around to opening, reading, and filing them, if they approve the need for the scissors their authorization sends it to Supply.

Arriving in Supply the process proceeds similar to what went on at Procurement.

After hours, days, weeks, or in our case maybe months the forms are checked, filed, approved if we are authorized to have scissors.
Once approved the requisition is sent to the proper section

of supply. Not everything is kept in one warehouse. Items are kept according to classification. Evidently scissors must be classified as a weapon. I say this because of the length of time for them to be approved.

The requisition arrives in the proper section and warehouse and after minutes, hours, days, weeks, they are taken from wherever they are kept in the building, placed in an envelope addressed to the office who requisitioned them.

The envelope containing the scissors are placed in Distribution and gradually make their way to our Information Office.

Total time was just over three months. I could have walked the forms through within two hours. Notice that I said "walked".

One Day a reporter, Bill Dupriest, from one of the Miami papers visited Captain Martin and while there read an article pointed out to him by the Captain then decided to cut it out and asked for scissors. Captain Martin told me to let him use our new scissors. The Captain told Bill to be careful with the scissors because he didn't know what we had to do to get them.

Being a reporter Bill asked what Captain Martin meant and the Captain told me to tell him all about acquiring the scissors. I did and Bill asked to use my typewriter and sat down and wrote an article poking fun at the length of time it took for a simple pair of scissors. The next day the article was in Bill's column in the newspaper.

Before Captain Martin arrived in the office the next day we were already called by the Colonel at the base Information Office wanting to know if we knew anything about the article in Bill's column.

Playing dumb I asked "What article? I haven't read that paper yet, sir." The Captain and I kept quiet. Some things are best left unsaid.

Reveille

Most soldiers hate the sound of the bugle at 0445, hours military time (4:45 AM) when this blessed event occurs. The word comes from the French word for "wake up". Taps signified the end of the day while reveille was the start of the day which alone tells why it was not the most popular musical offering for most American GIs.

As a veteran of military service to the country I love and have been blessed by God with the privilege to be an American living in the greatest country ever I give thanks to God regularly for this honor. And I do consider it an honor. Now that I have gotten older I think more about dying and eternity so it seems only natural for me the think of how I would like for my final arrangements to be carried out.

Both Alvin and Troy were tremendous trumpet players in high school. The local VFW would ask them each to play taps at the cemetery for burial of veterans. I have told them each to remain practiced and able to play their trumpets because I have a personal request for them to do for me. When they take me to the cemetery I want Alvin to play "Taps" signifying my day here on Earth is completed and it is time for rest.

Then immediately after Alvin finishes I want Troy to play "Reveille" signifying something different than what we learned in the military which was:

You've got to get up

You've got to get up

You've got to get up this morning

I wish for it to be perceived as:

Dad's gonna get up

Dad's gonna get up

Dad's gonna get up resurrection morning

On that day, resurrection day, like the Psalmist said in Chapter seventeen, verse fifteen, "As for me, I will behold thy face in righteousness: I shall be satisfied, when I awake, with thy likeness".

Life here is primarily a place to prepare for eternity.

That day will be my last reveille, one I anticipate and look forward to with all my heart and soul.

Made in the USA
Columbia, SC
08 July 2018